*For
Doug*

TRIPS, TRAVELS,
AND DREAMS

Michael Vaughn Palmer

TRIPS, TRAVELS, AND DREAMS

How LSD Saved Me

Michael Vaughn Palmer

TRIPS, TRAVELS, AND DREAMS
How LSD Saved Me
BY Michael Vaughn Palmer

michaelvaughnpalmer@outlook.com

© COPYRIGHT 2015
BY Michael Vaughn Palmer

ISBN: 978-1508530206

DESIGN & TYPOGRAPHY:
Fearless Literary Services • *www.fearlessbooks.com*

THE CONTENTS

ACKNOWLEDGEMENTS

I would like to thank the following people for assisting and encouraging me with the writing of my book: Susan Wilcox, Ana Marcelo, Marie Rowe, Bruce McCallister, Andrika Donovan, Janice Jordan, Jeramy "Moe" Moore, Barbara Jones, Robbie Cowden, Betty Denebeim, Deborah McKinzie, and Frank Burroughs.

I would also like to thank the San Bernardino City Library and the San Bernardino County Library, Highland Branch, where this book was written. The staff at both facilities were extremely friendly and helpful.

PROLOGUE

There are two interwoven stories in this book. The first one really happened.

While the first story begins in the unique and now nostalgic sixties, it was a wise man of considerable insight and awareness whose guidance led me from that time into a lifelong journey of learning. I'm sure that wise man, my friend Vassily, would agree that what was true back then is true today — if we would only see it. With deep thanks, I dedicate this book to him.

The second story is about the dream, and what the Captain taught me.

CHAPTER ONE

"For me it was a deep and mystical experience."
— DR. ALBERT HOFMANN, Discoverer of LSD-25

"LSD makes you more of what you are." — ALDOUS HUXLEY

"The only sensible thing to do with the human trap is to get out of it."
— VERNON HOWARD

THIS story begins with the ringing of my phone. Before it rang my life would have been considered relatively normal. I'd gone to public schools, worked in a steel mill, joined the navy, and was now attending an institution of "higher learning" in San José, California. I'd been doing all the things that were considered important, never questioning nor knowing that anything else was possible. Most of what had happened in my life was inconsequential — at least compared to what would take place after I answered the phone that day in 1966.

It was Pat calling. We'd met and become friends at a junior college in San Bernardino the year before. I pictured his round, grinning face and brown, brushy moustache that fit his jovial personality. Pat was unusual in that he always seemed to be aware of new ideas before they were even considered new.

"Hey, Pat. What's happenin'?"

"I'm livin' in San Francisco," Pat said, "and there's some far-out things happenin' up here. You gotta come visit me."

"Sure, man. I'll come up Saturday. Where do you live?"

"In Haight-Ashbury. It's a cool, old neighborhood by Golden Gate Park."

Pat gave me directions and said to be there about nine in the morning and to bring a sleeping bag if I wanted to spend the night. He added that we'd go over to the park and he'd show me what all the excitement was about.

It was a crisp, clear Saturday morning as I drove up Haight Street. Older two and three-story wood-framed houses lined both sides of the street. A grassy, tree-dotted Buena Vista Park appeared on the left, and then small stores and shops started to appear. Several people on the street stood out. First was a couple. The young man's hair was long — as long as his female companions. Both were wearing bell-bottom pants. Next was another long-haired guy with a wide grin, wearing old jeans and a T-shirt with a picture of a bearded man I'd seen on the cover flap of some rolling papers. A little farther on, six or seven similar-looking people were out in front of a small shop, talking and laughing.

Climbing the steps where Pat lived, I smiled and thought, *Haight-Ashbury sure looks like a well-tressed, happy place.*

I knocked. The door opened.

"Hey, Mike, good timing. I just woke up. Let me get a couple of things, and we'll take off for the park."

From the bit of daylight that squeezed through the edges of the shade-covered window, I was able to survey the room. A simple couch and table were the only furnishings. On the walls were three large posters. One featured a bright, exploding rainbow; another was a wild head shot of Albert Einstein; next to it was the beautiful actress Greta Garbo. When Pat returned, I was standing in front of Greta, ogling.

"Come on, Mike. The park's just a couple blocks away. I wasn't able to explain on the phone, but the far-out thing that's happenin' here is LSD. All the far-out people movin' into the Haight are all acid heads."

I'd read about LSD in a magazine, and a couple friends from school had mentioned it.

"Have you taken any yet?" Pat asked.

I shook my head.

"It's unbelievable! I've taken it six times since I moved here. The idea is to turn your friends and neighbors on to it. Better yet, the whole world. I picked up a couple of hits for us last night. Are you ready for a mind-expanding experience?"

"Sure," I said, intrigued. "It sounds interesting!"

Pat handed me a small plastic bag with a sugar cube in it, just like it was described in the magazine article. Sweet little blocks laced with LSD.

"This stuff is pure and strong. Just remember how to get back to my place in case we get separated."

Pat said the LSD would take effect in about thirty minutes. I let it dissolve in my mouth while we walked to the park and Pat told me about the Haight.

"Right up the street, the Psychedelic Shop just opened. They've got all kinds of cool stuff: posters, clothes, books, pipes, and there's always people out in front."

"Must've been the place that caught my eye."

"And tonight we can go over to the Fillmore Auditorium. Some music and stuff is happening there."

Golden Gate Park, with its trees, meadows and ponds, is a huge urban garden inside the otherwise paved-over big city. We walked about a quarter of a mile into it on a narrow dirt path, crossing a road and a few trails. At a small clearing we sat down on a fallen tree trunk and waited.

It's difficult to explain what happens on LSD. Ask anyone who's ever taken it, and they'll surely agree. But the description below is as

close as words can get to what I personally felt, saw and learned on
my first acid trip.

It started when I began to notice my breathing. Not the normal
operation of the lungs as they pulled in air and then expelled it. This
was a new awareness of small gasps centered in my solar plexus.
And my eyes kept blinking in an attempt to remain clearly focused.
There were sudden bursts of flashing lights and bright, clear colors.
Everything I looked at was quivering, like the shimmering waves of
heat that can be seen in the distance on a hot day. What felt like an
electrical current was slowly spreading through my body and mind.
Suddenly, each tree stood out in bright-green detail, the leaves were
amazingly clear and distinct, and the dirt that covered the ground
took on a beautiful, clean, earthy texture. Dark shadows were mixed
with bright beams of sunlight that sporadically shone through wide-
spread branches. I looked at my arms; the clarity of the skin and
hair was like seeing them through a magnifying glass. Sounds were
amplified and colors intensified. I had an overwhelming feeling of
susceptibility to everything that was taking place, and I had no choice
but to go along with it. My altered breathing allowed only one spoken
word: "Wow!"

I sat there in wide-eyed wonder for quite a while. I was glad no
one was out for a stroll in our special area, as it would have been difficult to communicate with anyone. It seemed as though my personality had departed and left whatever it was I was experiencing in
its place.

I looked at Pat and our minds were in sync. He was silently asking, "What do you think of this trip?" I didn't know what to think; I
didn't want to think. Everyday thoughts seemed so trivial and unneces-
sary. I was aware of a boundless freedom I'd never experienced before.

What came next wasn't from a thought; it was more like a sense
perception. This sensation expanded into a crystal-clear view of the

life I'd been living, and that's when I sat straight up. *Hey, somebody has tricked me!* Tricked us all into believing that our everyday life was so damned important and urgent, and it had to be lived according to a bunch of restrictive rules. And we'd allowed it to happen. We'd been duped by some Grand Trickster into thinking there was no alternative. We'd been hoodwinked, and the knowledge that we could be free from that narrow, limited life had been kept from us. I was seeing something I'd never seen before, and it was hilarious. I chuckled and looked at Pat, who was grinning from ear to ear. When our eyes met, the floodgate burst open, and uncontrollable laughter flowed out. We'd just been let in on the fraud of a lifetime, and the joke was on us. The funniest thing was that no one else knew it. Everyone was trying to be important and in such a big hurry in their quest for who-knows-what. And we'd been tricked into believing that was what we were supposed to be doing.

This unique realization wasn't manifested in words. It was a clear, silent perception. But I now understood what Pat meant when he said that taking LSD was a mind-expanding experience.

A few hours later, after the laugh session had relaxed into smiles, Pat and I decided to do some exploring. We struggled to our feet and began strolling through the park, enjoying all the trees and vegetation. We came to the back of a large building with several doors without handles. One of the doors opened and a couple stepped out. They held it open and asked us if we wanted to go in. We had no idea what was inside, but we nodded our heads in a "why not" gesture and stepped in.

The building was the home of the Steinhart Aquarium and contained a vast array of aquatic life, an existence different from our own but related because we were all alive. It was a sensory delight.

While peering into one large tank, I spotted a fish sporting a wild, yellow-paisley pattern. A quick verification from an information placard beside the tank confirmed I wasn't hallucinating. It was just the normal appearance of the naked fish. That was when I noticed that the inhibited humans all around had a colorful array of clothing hanging on them.

It was easy to empathize with the more natural life-forms in the tank. It wasn't an identity crisis, like a fish out of water, but I did feel like joining them for a swim!

It was during our exploration of the aquarium that Pat and I lost track of each other, but that was cool, since we'd arranged to meet up later at his place.

I returned to the park and tried to understand what had taken place earlier. It was like my mind had been shaken and I'd been forced to wake up. My vision had been refocused to see life in a new, transparent way. There were no urgent desires for anything, just a calm, peaceful sensation from an experience I'd never known before but knew I'd never forget. No results or conclusions were available, though; only a hint that I'd had a glimpse into a big mystic secret. It was the most astounding and hilarious thing that'd ever happened to me. I resolved then and there to learn everything I could about the experience. What did it mean, and what would it lead to? *What the hell was it all about?*

I met Pat back at his place, and that evening we headed to the Fillmore Auditorium. Music and light shows had recently started happening there and at the Avalon Ballroom. A poster on the wall next to the entrance of the three-story brick building announced in flowing script, *JEFFERSON AIRPLANE*.

Inside, rockin' music filled the air, and the colorful light show made the wall behind the stage look like a quivering, living organism. It was similar to what I'd experienced and seen earlier, and Pat agreed.

To the beat of the music, the gyrating, bouncing people made the floor shake like an Earthquake. Nobody was sitting down.

Several thousand bodies moved with the rhythm, and the light show pulsated right along with them. The alluring extravaganza called out and welcomed me. With a new sense of freedom, I laughed and danced right into the middle of it.

THAT eye-opening experience in San Francisco's Golden Gate Park was the turning point in my life. Returning to my old way of living was no longer an option. But what was next? There was one obvious place where the answer might be found: Haight-Ashbury. My move was a natural, easy transition. I checked out of school and moved to San Francisco.

LSD had opened a door to a new way of life. The growing number of like-minded people moving into Haight-Ashbury proved that I wasn't the only one experiencing this reaction. We'd been psychedelicized!

The new Haight-Ashbury was slowly expanding. The business area now featured a free medical clinic, the renovation of the Haight Theater into the Straight Theater, and everyone's favorite, the Diggers, who made meals from food thrown out by supermarkets. Even though they'd squeezed in between the regular neighborhood businesses, everyone got along.

The surrounding apartments and flats began to fill up with new arrivals as well. I moved into the communal flat on Cole Street where Pat and a fluctuating number of other people lived. Since we'd all had similar experiences, there were many expansive discussions on what exactly was happening. I wanted to know why my mind all of a sudden perceived things differently and clearly while under the influence of LSD. What exactly were these revelations?

I read everything available on the subject. There were studies underway at several universities and medical facilities on the effects and uses of LSD, but very little was written for the layperson. I read the botanists, anthropologists and philosophers who had studied and experimented with the various psychoactive plants in South America, the psilocybin "magic" mushrooms in Mexico, and the religious use of peyote cactus by Native Americans in the Southwest.

During my search, the name Dr. Timothy Leary kept showing up. He'd been experimenting with LSD at Harvard University, where he was a professor and research psychologist. I'd met several people from back East who'd taken LSD in one of his studies or had heard him lecture on the subject; they all spoke very highly of him. I read what was available by Leary, and he kept referring to mystical, religious and spiritual experiences while high on acid. I came across the same references in a revealing lecture he'd delivered at a meeting of Lutheran psychologists, in conjunction with the seventy-first Annual Convention of the American Psychological Association, in August 1963. In an experiment conducted by Dr. Leary, sixty-nine Christian, Jewish, and Eastern religious leaders had taken LSD. Seventy-five percent claimed they'd had a religious experience, and over half of them said it was the deepest religious experience of their lives.

I understood the mystical aspect, but I didn't think I'd ever had a spiritual or religious experience. That was until Leary tied it in with experiencing and realizing the truth and the freedom it provided. What he'd said finally dawned on me: that glimpse of truth, when seen or realized on LSD, was a mystical, spiritual, and religious revelation.

Through the Haight-Ashbury word-of-mouth information mill, I learned there was going to be a big function in Golden Gate Park. The Human Be-In/A Gathering of the Tribes was the first-ever get-together of its kind. Everyone would meet in a big open meadow to hear some music — Jefferson Airplane and several other bands were to play — and listen to prominent guest speakers. I knew I'd attend because one of them would be none other than Dr. Timothy Leary.

Dynamic Haight-Ashbury had become densely populated with free-spirited acid heads. They were dubbed "hippies" by Herb Caen, a popular San Francisco newspaper columnist. The rest of the media called them "the peace and love generation." It was apt as it described the feelings one had while stoned on LSD — any conflict was out of the question, and making love was high on the priority list.

A lot of those hippies showed up in the park on January 14, 1967. I don't know what the actual count was, but my estimate was forty or fifty thousand people. Also in attendance was the underground LSD chemist Owsley Stanley. He was handing out samples of his effective and latest creation called White Lightning.

It was a mild, sunny day with scattered high clouds as I wove through the crowd spread out in front of the small stage. I worked my way to the front and found a small patch of turf to sit on. There were some guest speakers, like beatnik poet Lawrence Ferlinghetti and the chanting Allen Ginsberg.

Then Leary was introduced. He commenced with the seven famous words that would become the maxim of hippies around the world:

"Turn on, tune in, and drop out."

His edification brought a cheer from the crowd. I laughed, recalling my old, pre-LSD lifestyle, and now understood exactly what he meant.

Being comfortable with all the recent changes in my life, I decided to expand them further. There were some unique learning opportunities being offered in the local alternative newspapers. The most interesting was for an introductory course in yoga. It was to be held at the instructor's home in the Richmond District.

The class started with eight of us being given thin pads to lie on. The instructor, a wispy middle-aged man, first demonstrated a stretching exercise and then helped us as we attempted to imitate it. I felt more relaxed as we went through about twenty of the movements and postures. They had cool names like Half Moon, Eagle Stand, Heron, Cobra and, my favorite, Salute to the Sun. It was the most relaxed I'd ever been, and I was wide-awake and alert. The instructor promised that frequent practice would make us more limber, relaxed and in control of our bodies, minds and lives. I walked out into the cool night air, poured myself behind the wheel of my car, and decided that I should do Salute to the Sun as often as possible.

Living in the bustling Haight was like being in a free-form fantasy: no one cared what you looked like or what you did, and everyone was friendly. My favorite pastime was watching the happy locals. They came from states as far away as New York and Florida, and from countries like England and Canada. There were artists who created wildly colorful, psychedelic art and inspired light shows that mimicked the kaleidoscopic acid experience. There were musicians who played the San Francisco sound, appropriately called "acid rock." They were provided with music showcases like the Family Dog Productions at the Avalon Ballroom, Bill Graham's Fillmore Auditorium, the Straight Theater, and the smaller Matrix club. There were writers who filled the pages of *The Oracle* and other underground publications with stories, poetry, and LSD philosophy.

But my fondest memories were of the vigorous people who made Haight-Ashbury the hip place to be. From men and women wearing eclectic and colorful clothing, to their babies with tie-dyed diapers, it seemed like everyone was turned on. The Haight was alive with the vibrant feeling of transformation from the old to the new. It was an astonishing place to be!

One acid-filled weekend, my friend Guitar Michael and I went to the Monterey Pop Festival. We camped on the football field at the local college and were woken up Saturday morning by live music from Country Joe and the Fish. Our weekend, though, was high-lighted by a mind-blowing performance by Jimi Hendrix. It was such an unforgettable experience that my friend decided to dedicate his life to his guitar, hence the name Guitar Michael.

During my mercurial stay in San Francisco, I still had a few con-ventional jobs. I worked at the post office for a while and for a friend who managed a temporary-employment agency. I also managed a rock band and worked with Tall Gary's psychedelic light show production.

The rock band and the light show took me on a visit to Portland, Oregon, which I thought was behind the times. After living in the Haight, it seemed to me that every other place appeared to be waiting for its own psychedelic revolution to take place.

During the visit to Portland, I managed to have a run-in with the law.

Back in San Francisco, I was part of a loose-knit group of a dozen friendly people who traded marijuana and LSD among themselves. One of them was from Portland, and she said a friend of hers would love to get some grass from California. I agreed to help, and she gave me a few bags of the herb to take to him. She also said I could stay with another friend of hers while in Portland.

Upon my arrival, I left my suitcase with the pot at the home where I was staying and went to take care of business concerning the band. That evening I returned to find the front door wide open, the house ransacked, and my suitcase gone. The police had paid a visit. I called the guy the pot was intended for. He'd heard about what had happened and invited me to stay at his place.

The band's gig and light show at the Crystal Ballroom went without a hitch. Before I could leave, though, the police came to arrest the guy I was staying with for some minor infraction.

In my shirt pocket was a Marlboro box with a joint inside. The police found it, and I was arrested for possession of one joint. After quickly being released, I met with an attorney. He assured me that the charge would probably be dropped, so I went back to San Francisco.

Back in The City, the Haight was slowly changing from the idyllic place it had been. Moving in were a growing number of unsmiling faces that were into hard drugs. There was also an influx of greedy businesspeople who came to exploit what was taking place for money. The outside world was infringing on the LSD community. Those were the two main reasons why the new-lifestyle residents began to move out. Many headed north to Marin, Mendocino, and Sonoma Counties and some to other areas of San Francisco. I moved to the city's Mission District.

The increase in experimentation with LSD across the country was continuing. I'd guesstimate that over a million people had taken LSD at this point, and every day more people were joining those who were openly flaunting the establishment by "dropping out" of society. This was unacceptable to the powers in control of running the societal machine, and their response was obvious. The governmental authorities got help from the media to put an end to what they saw as a menacing threat.

They came up with several ways to stem the perilous problem: scare tactics and laws based on ignorance. First they came up with a story about someone who thought he could fly and had jumped out of a window. The vague story stated that psychologists claimed it was a normal reaction, and they insinuated it could happen to anyone who experimented with LSD. It was not convincing, however, to the million who'd been through the mind-expanding experience.

There was another falsehood that the government-influenced media used. It was a claim that taking LSD initiated chromosomal damage and caused babies to be born deformed and demented. There was never a single report of this ever happening. Both assertions were phony, but the scare tactics were working.

The government authorities then made possession of LSD illegal and placed it in the group of Schedule 1 hard-core drugs. To say that LSD was the same as heroin showed ignorance of the subject. But those in control were afraid, and a large part of what they did worked.

The scare tactics and laws had substantially diminished experimentation with LSD, but for me the deed was done. I had a better understanding of what had happened during my LSD experiences. The remaining question was, to what and where would it lead me?

CHAPTER TWO

*"Here is the test to find whether your mission on Earth
is finished: if you're alive, it isn't."* — RICHARD BACH

*"It is not known precisely where angels dwell —
whether in the air, the void, or the planets."* — VOLTAIRE

*"The self is subordinate to you, yet on
the other hand rules you."* — ROSINUS

T HE other story in this book takes place in my subconscious. It's
a dream, a fable of the learning path that LSD invited me on.
It's a subliminal tale of a journey through the far reaches of the universe with my learned guide, the Captain.

Although he has a number of glowing titles, the Captain performs just a single function. He helps living beings when they've fully realized how to free themselves from the restrictive mental and physical plane of existence on their respective planets. He assists them when they ascend and return home to true reality. The Captain is a celestial guide, and I've been allowed to accompany him.

LSD ushered me to a portal to the other side and the inception of the dream. A clear flow of energy carried me through that open door and into a large seat as plush as a soft cloud. I felt at ease as I looked over at the Captain. He looked like some kind of angelic sorcerer. There was an easygoing smile on his wizened face, he wore a comfortable white jumpsuit, and he made things happen with a snap of his fingers and a hearty, unique laugh. He said the space-traveling ve-hicle we were in was for my comfort. I wondered how he got around otherwise. I always meant to ask, but there were more important things to learn.

The Captain had already received his latest orders and was on his way when I joined him. He handed me a printout of where we were going. By the time I'd finished reading the navigating coordinates IC2 and our destination — the planet DDiipplloooppiiaa, where all of the inhabitants have double vision — we were there.

I watched as the Captain made sure all in the group had ascended; then I said to him, "The eyesight on that planet is a doppelganger. When they have a beautiful sunset, everybody gets to see it twice at the same time. But we did assist forty — or was it eighty? — happy as-cenders, and it went without a hitch."

"It did go smoothly. But you've got to be alert. Something un-expected could happen and an important decision might have to be made."

"I'll bet you've seen it all," I said in awe.

"Speaking of seeing," said the Captain, "while we're in this area I want to cruise over to sector JST1."

"The map shows that JST1 has just one inhabited planet. It's called Earth. What's so important about it?" I asked, not remembering a single thing about my life there.

"My first visit to the planet was unusual. So I did some research on the inhabitants, and I like to keep up with anything new that's going on there. Have you ever seen any Earthlings?"

"No, can't say as I have."

"I'll put some pictures of them on the screen."

"Wow! They're all wearing strange-looking hats," I said.

"Those aren't hats," said the Captain. "That's hair."

"They put hair on their heads?"

"No, Michael, it grows there."

"Why does hair grow out of the top of their heads?"

"It's the way they've physically evolved. Hair used to cover their entire body, but they've lost most of it. However, as you noticed, some still grows out of the top of their heads."

"Why do they all look so different?"

"They cut their hair into different shapes, and some color it and kind of glue it into various forms."

"Why in the world do they do that?" I asked between laughs.

"They think it makes them more attractive to the opposite sex. This is where the psychological conditioning of the Earthlings gets complex. To make it easier to understand, I'll explain some of their mental history."

"How far back do you have to go?"

"About four million Earth years should do. But it's important for you to understand that time and space aren't what they appear to be. There'll be a surprise at the end of this story, and I'll explain what I mean."

"Cool. I like surprises," I said.

"I'll start when evolution was nearly finished molding them into their current physical appearance. They'd been living in a tropical jungle on a land they call Africa. Just outside it were vast forests and grasslands. It was a garden paradise with an abundant food supply, so the evolving Earthlings migrated.

"One of the many animals available was wild cattle, and they provided an odd benefit. Among the edible plants was a unique mushroom, and it grew where those wild cattle left their dung."

"Bull shit!" I interjected.

"What?"

"Sorry, Captain. I meant 'bull shit,' not 'bullshit.' Everyone knows manure is good for plant growth."

"Thank you," said the Captain with a laugh, "for that clarification.

"This mushroom was unique because it was psychoactive and hallucinogenic. The chemical reaction it had on the Earthlings' brains provided immediate benefits and enduring long-term effects. A direct advantage was that their awareness and vision improved, which enhanced their gathering and hunting abilities. They also became peaceful and caring. More importantly, the psychoactive effects initiated mystical wonder on the planet."

"Captain," I said, enthralled by what I was hearing, "they had plenty to eat, were friendly and loving, and experienced holy hallucinations. Sounds like paradise to me."

"Nevertheless," said the amused Captain, "here's what's mind-boggling. During the next three million years their brain tripled in size, and that growth provided a new mental function.

"The Earthlings, or humans as I'll sometimes refer to them, started living in cooperative settings. Communicating information verbally began to be important. That meant a need to store words and symbols in their brains, or more precisely, their minds. They needed to develop an expanding memory."

"So they're born without any memory?" I asked.

"None they are aware of," said the Captain. "But they have a preexisting mental memory. Everything from their past lives is concealed in their subconscious, and a plan for their ensuing life is there, as well.

"What happens is a tiny part of their minds begins to reflect back on itself. This small mental fragment commences to file away and recall words and symbols. It acts as the overseer of memorization.

"This is the forerunner of the remarkable memory of the present-day Earthlings. It records and recalls information quickly and accurately. And it's the main reason the humans are so creative and inventive. The larger and more complex their memory gets, the more important the overseer becomes. It then commences to use the same words it files away in memory to describe its own activity."

"So what's the problem?" I asked.

"What I've explained is the way the overseer files away factual information. At first I didn't think it was a problem. Then I looked a little deeper.

"From the moment they're born, the mind receives outside influences. They're told who they are, what they are, what behavior is acceptable and objectionable, and, more importantly, what to believe. Their mind is psychologically conditioned to conform so there won't be anyone who believes or acts differently in their societal group."

"It's like a human computer being programmed," I said.

"The small mental fragment, using words, then creates the thinker with a thought, and names it 'I.' Thought has created the thinker, rather than the thinker creating thought. And there is no 'I' because it's only a thought as well.

"The humans mistakenly call the fictitious 'I' the self, or ego, and so begins the misleading process of self-consciousness. The ego actually oversees the entire process and wants it to appear that the outside world has made the humans what they are. But it's a trick and a problem.

"With that in mind," said the Captain, "new orders are ready."

He snapped his fingers and bellowed out his unique laugh, and our next assignment was in his hand.

"Here's the printout, Michael. Where are we going this time?"

"We're heading for the navigation coordinates A2Z and the planet...uh, the planet...uh, I can't pronounce it."

"Let me see it," said the Captain. "Oh, sure, we're going to the planet Abrgostukfilbnetjpydz."

"I still can't pronounce it," I said. "Let's just say we're off to the coordinates A2Z and the alphabet planet!"

CHAPTER THREE

*"The true value of a human being is determined by the measure
and sense in which he has attained liberation from the self."*
— ALBERT EINSTEIN

*"Man's entire problem is that he is unaware of
being unaware."* — VERNON HOWARD

"If you think you're free, there's no escape possible."
— RAM DASS

"When the student is ready, the teacher will appear."
— ZEN PROVERB

THE Mission District of San Francisco proved to be an ideal place
to live. I could zip over to Haight-Ashbury or any other part of
the city and then escape back to my hideaway.

While out strolling on a foggy morning, I found myself back
on Haight Street. I came to an abrupt halt, as out of the gray mist
appeared the bright face of a girl I knew. Her name was Flower,
which aptly described her perennial smile.

Flower excitedly told me she was studying astrology and offered
to configure my astrological chart. She jotted down my pertinent
birth data — place, date and time — and we agreed to meet back at
the same spot in the afternoon.

At the appointed time, Flower was waiting with a couple of
sheets of paper in her hand.

"I hope it's correct," she said. "I've only done one other chart, so I can't guarantee it. There's an astrology bookshop over on Polk Street. You can ask them to check it."

The following day I visited the shop on Polk to see what the astrology thing was all about. There was a man sitting at a small table when I ambled in. I told the woman behind the counter the story behind my chart and handed it to her.

"You're a Sagittarius," she said. "First, let me ask our resident psychic what he thinks. Oh, Vassily," she sang out to the guy at the table, who looked more like the average man on the street than a psychic. "Would you be kind enough to tell me if you can pick up anything from this chart?"

He held it for five seconds and then said matter-of-factly, "There's too much fire!"

The lady nodded and said she'd do a quick assessment of the chart to see if it contained any errors.

While waiting I browsed through their books and came across the *I Ching* or *Book of Changes*, with a foreword by Carl Jung, and decided to buy it. At the counter, the woman also had my chart.

"There was an error in the calculation. Your friend had Leo as the ascendant, which is a fire sign. After the correction it moves up a sign to Virgo, which is an Earth sign.

"Oh, Vassily," she warbled again. "There was a fire sign in the chart that wasn't supposed to be there! You were right!"

He gave her a look that conveyed, *Well, of course I was!*

I strolled over to where the man sat and thanked him.

With a hearty laugh he said, "Oh, it was nothing."

I had a strange feeling I'd heard that otherworldly laugh before.

"You're a psychic," I commented.

"Oh, you noticed," he said with the same lively laugh. "I give tarot card readings here in the shop. I use the cards because they give me a clearer vision for my clients."

"Maybe I should have a reading?" I suggested.

Vassily quietly gazed at me for ten seconds and then said, "No, you don't need one right now. You're in a learning state, but when that begins to change you might want one. Hey, it's my lunchtime. There's a good sandwich shop across the street. Want to go have a bite?"

Across the street over lunch I asked Vassily about his name, as I'd never heard it before.

"As a boy, I had the ability to see the future and to do things no one else could do. As a young man, I decided to leave my so-called normal life and return to that. Changing my name initiated it. Since I have an affinity with things Russian, like their patron saint, the name I chose was Vassily."

"I understand what you did," I said. "I didn't change my name, but I did leave the old me behind to become, well…I'm not exactly sure."

With an understanding smile, Vassily said, "Why don't we get together tonight? I have to get back to the shop for some appointments, but here's my address. Come by about seven, and we can talk some more."

And that was the beginning of a friendship with an amazing man from whom I learned a great deal.

I met with Vassily that night and many other times over the next couple of years. I was constantly amazed at the vast array of subjects he'd mastered. He spoke about ten languages and could even read and write Sanskrit.

He was a master chef and would often work at a French restaurant in Sausalito. He excelled at Japanese cuisine, too.

Vassily was also an operatic tenor and loved to sing. He was well known at the best piano bars in town, and he always received a standing ovation for his singing.

I was at his apartment one evening, looking through his collection of books, when I came across one on wine making. On the inside cover the author had written that he considered Vassily the most knowledgeable person on wine making that he'd ever met.

He was also adept at acupuncture and taught a class on the subject. He was a hypnotist, a professional psychic, a talented sculptor and a mycologist. He had even invented a new stitch in crocheting. And the list goes on.

But more important than all of the many things that Vassily knew, he was a deeply spiritual person. He had great insights into life. Every time we got together, no matter what subject our conversation started on, we always ended up talking about the metaphysical secrets of life.

Being befriended by Vassily enabled me to do a lot of interesting things: dining at obscure international cafés; meeting people from foreign lands; being backstage when he sang in a production of *Madame Butterfly*; attending his favorite Yule celebration at the Russian Orthodox church. And we were forever going on long walks to different parts of the city, looking for the unusual.

Vassily also had a piercing sense of humor, so we laughed a lot. He often joked about the hilarious absurdity of everyday life. He believed everyone could use a good gut-wrenching laugh at themselves and the way they lived.

In one of our first conversations on the subject, I asked him, "What's wrong? Why is everyone so screwed up?"

"It's a lack of awareness," he professed. "People are completely under the influence of their ego and psychologically conditioned mind. What they have to do is free themselves from their false self and gain awareness of their higher mind."

I didn't comprehend what he meant. However, it would be

brought up many times in our later discussions.

I told Vassily about my experiments with LSD and the decision to drop out of the life dictated by society. His reply provided me with an insightful lesson.

"You do yourself a great disservice by doing that," he advised. "It means that, by exclusion, you still allow society to determine how you'll live and what you'll do. The secret is to be free to function in it but not become a part of it. In other words, be in it but not of it. Don't become psychologically addicted to society and dependent on it. That way, you can go into and out of it any time you wish. Use it for whatever you want, whenever you want, instead of it controlling and using you all the time.

"Your experiments with LSD gave you a glimpse of what higher-mind awareness is like. Now you can learn other ways to attain it.

"For example," he continued, "there's a game you can play that'll raise your awareness. I call it Spaceman. It takes a great deal of attention to sustain it. You start by pretending you're from another planet and have just arrived here on Earth to study the lives of the Earthlings. You don't know what to expect because you've never been here before, and you have to figure out what they're doing and why they do the things they do. It's a great learning experience and, at times, hilarious. People do some funny things, and they don't even know it. It'll make you laugh at them, at yourself, at everything. It's very therapeutic, but more importantly it'll introduce you to a new understanding of awareness and a new way to look at life."

I thought, *That sounds vaguely familiar.*

"As for LSD," Vassily said, "I took it once…"

I was ready, waiting to hear about his mind-expanding experience.

"… and nothing happened. The people I was with got high, but nothing happened to me. I was just the same as I am now. Maybe I'm just naturally stoned all the time!"

Natural or unnatural, I saw Vassily do astonishing things.

The first time I witnessed his magical ability, it was almost comical. He suggested that we go hunting for some morel mushrooms. Conditions weren't right, he admitted, but it was a good excuse to get out of the city. We drove north for an hour or so before arriving at a mountainous, pine tree-covered area with a lake nearby. We hiked through the woods all morning, with Vassily pointing out and collecting numerous herbs and other edible plants.

Early in the afternoon, we ended up at the lake. There were a lot of people on the shore, but as we walked by the water's edge only one man was fishing.

"Are you catchin' anything?" Vassily asked.

"Nope, not a thing." The angler shook his head. "They're not bitin'. This morning they were, but not now. There's a fishing tournament today. That's why there're so many people around. They have prizes for the biggest catch. But since they aren't bitin' no one's fishin'. I love to fish, so I'm just down here goin' through the motions."

"Have you got any other lures?" Vassily asked.

"Yeah," said the fisherman. "Take a look. I've got about a dozen here."

"Try this one," Vassily suggested, pointing at a lure.

"Sure, why not?" replied the man, shrugging nonchalantly. As the fisherman changed lures, Vassily squatted down, drew something in the sand, and then stood up again.

"On the seventh cast, you'll catch a fish," Vassily said while looking out over the water.

On his seventh cast, just a few seconds after the lure hit the water, wham! A strike! The man's fishing rod bent at a ninety-degree angle.

"What the hell? I got one! And it's big, too. How'd you do that?"

The fish was finally landed and in his hands.

"Wow, it's a beaut! How'd that happen? It's one of the biggest fish of the day! I've got to get it over to the scales! Wow! What the... How'd you...I've got to...I'll be back!"

I turned to Vassily and mimicked, "How'd you do that?"

"A simple explanation is difficult, to say the least, but I'll try," my friend said with a smile.

"To change something outside yourself, you have to change it in your mind first. There are no spoken words, just awareness. Using the connection with my higher mind, I clearly see that the outcome has already taken place. Next, I put my personal sign on it and let it go. Truthfully, it's deeper and more personal, but that's the simplest explanation."

And I believed him, because I saw it happen!

"You can learn something similar," Vassily said. "It's a first step in developing your higher mind. The secret is you can attract anything you're in need of, at any time, by not interfering. Don't speculate on what you think you need or want. The outcome doesn't come to you through your conditioned thought process. That has to be set aside so your higher mind can provide for you. Just know that whatever you are in true need of at that particular time has already come to you. Then drop all concern, and let it materialize for you."

I saw him use his magic other times, too. Many of them involved a personal healing situation.

One time he encountered a depressed young man who'd been told he needed emergency kidney-stone surgery. Vassily calmed him and made arrangements to stay with him for two weeks. Every couple of hours, he was given a cup of a special tea concoction. After fourteen days, the young man returned to his doctor, who was dumbfounded. The stones no longer required surgery, as they'd dissolved and disappeared.

Vassily taught in a manner that forced me to prove that what I'd learned was true, that it worked, and that it could also be applied on other levels. This was especially so when he assisted me with a personal problem.

I'd started smoking cigarettes at fifteen because it was the cool thing to do. Although I didn't smoke much, it was a problem because I had to smoke every day, and I didn't like that. Vassily saw my dilemma with the addiction and offered another learning solution.

He began with the profound statement, "In any struggle between will and imagination, imagination always wins. In using will you have to admit there's a problem, and that verifies and sustains the problem. But when using imagination, you eliminate it by merely imagining the problem doesn't exist, never has, and never will, thus eliminating the struggle. Like I told you before, to change something outside yourself you must change it inside first."

I imagined there was no such thing as tobacco and cigarettes, so how could I be addicted to something that didn't exist. I imagined them right out of existence, and it must have worked, because I'm no longer dependent on whatever it was I was apparently addicted to.

Vassily emphasized that every time I learned a metaphysical truth, I'd be presented with a situation to see if I'd fully realized it.

"You'll be tested to see if you've learned it by rote and filed it away in memory where your conditioned mind can trick you into thinking you know it. Or if you've realized the metaphysical truth and are able to successfully apply it."

AFTER living in San Francisco for three years, I began contemplating leaving, what with the demise of the Haight and all. I was wondering where I might go when it appeared the decision had been made for me.

One evening there was a knock on my front door. It was two plainclothes police officers from the Fugitive Division of the San

Francisco Police Department. They had a Portland, Oregon, warrant for my arrest on two counts of possession of marijuana.

"Is Michael Palmer here?" they asked.

"No," I instinctively answered. Then, thinking just as fast, I continued, "He works nights at the post office and won't be home until tomorrow morning."

"You fit his description. Do you have any identification?"

There's something to good timing. Two months before I'd read an article in an underground magazine on how to obtain a driver's license under an assumed name. I had no need for one — at least that's what I'd thought — but I'd gone through the steps just to see if it worked, and it had.

I showed them my newly acquired license and said, "Mike told me about something that happened to him in Portland a long time ago, but he thought the whole thing had been dropped."

"Not according to these papers," said the officer. "Anyway, here's my card. Have him call me tomorrow and we'll try to get this thing cleared up, one way or another."

Next morning, I called the police officer and said, "My roommate told me you guys were by my place last night looking for me."

The officer on the phone laughed and said, "Yeah, and we sure scared the hell out of him!"

There was no doubt they knew it was me. Some San Francisco cops are cool, and these two definitely were.

"I thought that charge had been dropped," I said honestly.

The officer, still chuckling, said, "Look, we're busy enough as it is. Here's the phone number in Portland. Call 'em and try to get it straightened out. But let us know what they say."

My call to Portland confirmed that the warrant was real. I didn't understand why there were two charges, but they wouldn't give me any additional information over the phone.

I called the San Francisco police officer back and said, "It's a shock to me. I'll have to go up and get it straightened out. I'll need a couple of weeks to get everything arranged, though."

"Sure," said the cool cop. "We won't hassle you. Just give us a call before you leave, and hey, good luck!"

I called Vassily, and he said to come right over. He could see I was stressed.

"I guess it's time for that tarot card reading we discussed back when."

He laid the cards out on a table and sat there contemplating them for a few minutes.

"This is a very significant and consequential moment," he said. "You've learned some of the basics of metaphysics that lead to a higher-mind awareness. You haven't understood everything, but important new lessons are now in your subconscious. As you learn them, they'll provide realizations and advanced metaphysical abilities throughout your life. This process isn't easy, as the ego is well entrenched in your mind and will obstruct your efforts at every turn. The cards also show that you'll be directed to locations and situations where your metaphysical learning will take place. Just remember that developing your higher mind is the most important endeavor in your life.

"This reading," Vassily continued, "also reveals something very important I have to tell you. There will be two very long and extremely difficult tests for you that will take place later in your life. In the first one, all of the metaphysical truths you've learned will be hidden from you, and you'll have to prove that you deserve to get them back. I can't impress on you enough the importance of making it through this test, as you may lose everything — and I mean everything. It's a necessary step that you'll have to do without assistance, to be allowed to continue learning.

"Concerning your more immediate problem in Portland, I see no reason why you shouldn't go up there and resolve it."

Vassily paused, looked me straight in the eyes, and in a monotone voice slowly said, "There will be nothing there to bother you! This change" — he resumed in his normal voice — "will turn out well for you. It'll lead to some new opportunities that you'll thoroughly enjoy. So there's no reason for you not to go to Portland. Besides," he said with a big smile, "I can come up and visit you!"

Vassily's words were reassuring, but I had to admit I was still concerned about the outcome of my legal entanglement. Then I smiled and wondered what the new opportunities would be.

CHAPTER FOUR

*"Classical Anthropology distinguishes between religion and magic
by saying that religion involves a deity whom man implores
while magic involves forces which man commands."*
— MARGARET J. FIELD

*"Psychedelic experiences, shamanic experiences are penetrations
into a higher dimension."* — TERRENCE McKENNA

"I STILL can't pronounce the name of that planet," I said while watching it recede from view.

"You mean Abrgostukfilbnetjpydz," the Captain said melodically.

"I understand circumstances for inhabitants are different on each planet, but those poor folks have to overcome a language that defies phonetics. I like to hear you say it, though. I'd also like to hear more about planet Earth."

"OK. This next phase will be about their religion. There were two activities that unfolded in the garden paradise. One was a shamanic healing practice, and the other was religious worship. I'll start with shamanism," said the Captain, shifting to his storytelling voice. "Those who experienced the deepest realizations from the mushrooms initiated the practice. They understood how mental energy could be used to one's advantage. Those skillful at using the power became a combination of shaman and medicine man for their cultural group. They were able to divine the future, manipulate events that affected the welfare of their people, and cure the sick by administering healing herbs.

"This causal world was also accessible by repetitive, intense physical activity that produced a trancelike state. Examples like intense dancing, rhythmic breathing, chanting, fasting and meditation were used. As the shaman became more skilled, the reliance on these practices diminished. The adept shaman could tap into this mental state with the inscription of his personal sign, which was a quick access key to the mental realm."

"Captain, I have a question."

"Sure, I can answer anything."

"I understand how abstinence or continuous physical activity could modify awareness. They sort of force one to view things from an altered mental state. But the question I have is about the mushrooms. How do they create a state where everything is perceived so clearly?"

"It's their psychologically conditioned thoughts that created the thinker and the 'I,' and the entire process is controlled by the ego. The main effect of mushrooms is dissolving the ego. This allows the individual to experience a state that's free from psychological conditioning. It's temporary, though, as the effects last only a short time."

"But, Captain, there has to be a way Earthlings can free themselves permanently. Otherwise there's no hope for 'em."

"There are ways they can free themselves and return to true reality. I'll tell you about the ultimate liberating process at the end of this story. That's also when your surprise happens!"

"Thanks for the warning. I've got another question. Could shamans really predict the future, influence events and heal the sick?"

"They must have done all that," said the Captain. "If they hadn't been able to, interest in them would have disappeared. In fact, there are still shamans on Earth that have the ability to do all those things, and in some cases more. To call shamanism a religion, though, is a bit of a stretch. There's a quasi-religious overtone, but it's really a personal experience for the shaman and a cultural phenomenon for the people they served."

"You also mentioned a religious activity," I said. "Is it related to culture, too?"

"All religions on Earth have a cultural origin. As for the first worshipping religion practiced by the Earthlings, I think you'll find it interesting, too. But before you hear about it, new orders are coming in."

The Captain snapped his fingers and laughed, and a paper with our next assignment was in his hand.

"We're going to coordinates 4NOT and a planet called Kontrary. It's where all the inhabitants have conflicting opinions. So we get to assist fifteen Kontrarians who have quit arguing and are ready to return to pure reality."

CHAPTER FIVE

*"Leave all things to take their natural course,
and do not interfere."* — LAO-TZU

"Nothing endures but change." — HERACLITUS

"The journey of life is like a man riding a bicycle."
— WILLIAM GOLDING

IT WAS 1969, and a dilemma awaited me in Portland. Even though Vassily had provided psychic reassurance, I was still bothered by negative thoughts and anxiety.

I put on my best smile and met with an affable attorney, one of the best in Portland. He was intrigued with the case. With a brief phone call, he learned that the second charge was for some marijuana found in a suitcase containing papers with my name. But it was a strange case, he added. I had to be convicted of possession of the one joint, since it was found on my person, before I could be convicted of the second charge of possession of the pot found in the suitcase.

The day I appeared in court is permanently imprinted in the legal record book, and I'll never forget it, either. My attorney and I were sitting at one table, and on another table was the evidence: a Marlboro box and a suitcase. The prosecutor was describing the case to the judge, but his emphasis was on the marijuana found in the suitcase.

The judge reminded him that his case depended on what was in my possession. Then he said, "I'd like to see that evidence."

The prosecuting attorney picked up the Marlboro box, opened it, and looked inside. It was empty!

He came up with a lame excuse for the missing contents, but the judge didn't buy it.

The robed gentleman sitting at the front of the courtroom looked at me, smiled and said, "Case dismissed!"

In wide-eyed reverence, I stared at the empty Marlboro box and heard Vassily conjuring, "There will be nothing there to bother you!"

This reemphasized the validity of Vassily's metaphysics; everything I was learning deserved my attention and respect.

I recalled an exercise he had me do back in San Francisco. We were at a busy downtown intersection, with a double cable-car crossing. He told me to cross the street, back and forth, for several minutes without looking down. When he asked me what I'd learned, I had no answer.

"As you crossed the street," Vassily pointed out, "you never once tripped or stepped on the tracks. Now watch everyone else try to cross it."

Pedestrians were looking down, up, left, right, and down again. They were shuffling, staggering and stumbling to avoid the tracks while crossing the busy street.

"That's a basic, simple example," Vassily continued, "of how your higher-mind awareness works. It'll safely guide you and provide for you, as long as you don't interfere."

With my life in a mellower state, I decided to check out what was happening in Portland. There was a small music scene: one decent rock band, a good blues band, a talented old-time jug band, and a great symphony orchestra. But there were very few places to hear live music.

I came across an article in the local underground newspaper about a noncommercial radio station. I tuned to it and heard some strange, melodic music. The announcer said, "That was gamelan gong music from Bali, Indonesia. This is K-B-O-O, ninety-point-seven FM, noncommercial, listener-supported radio in Portland."

The article said the station needed volunteers, so I called Roger, the program director. He wanted to start a block-programming format and publish a program guide for subscribers, and he needed help doing it. He also asked me to take the test for an FCC Third-Class Radio Telephone Operator License.

Vassily had taught me a learning method based on his favorite tarot card, the Moon. He called it *crepusculum,* which meant twilight or the balance between sleep and wakefulness. It's a reflective, meditative state similar to self-hypnosis. I'd relax, close my eyes and go over the information for the test. It worked, as I easily passed and got my license.

The station was located in two small rooms in the dark, dusty basement of a downtown building. It was real underground radio that broadcast diverse, aesthetic music and interesting information programs. I informed Roger I'd do anything to help. With nervous excitement I started doing the regular announcing duties on Tuesday and Thursday night and, my favorite, a blues music show on Sunday night.

I'd been at KBOO a month when Roger told me the station manager was leaving. The board of directors at KRAB, our sister station in Seattle, which helped KBOO get its operating license, asked Roger to take over as manager. He wanted to set up a board of directors, register as a nonprofit and tax-exempt organization, move out of the basement and get a more powerful transmitter.

"As the new manager," Roger added, "I'd like you to be the new program director. I think you'd be good at it."

A week later I took over a job with a title and very little pay. Yet I remain thankful for the outlook on life I learned from the station. It was a community operation whose philosophy was "no philosophy," characterized by a program called "Open Forum." It was available to any person, group, or organization to speak on any subject: politics from the left or right; social concepts, pro and con; and religious and antireligious views. There was one condition: if speakers verbally attacked anyone, we'd allow the other person an equal amount of broadcast time to address and counter the assertions.

Vassily had warned me about the false self taking recognition for accomplishments. He explained, "The ego is very tricky. It'll say, 'Look what I did! Look what I made happen!' When, in fact, its noninvolvement allowed what happened to manifest."

One evening I was at Goose Hollow Inn having a beer. The guy next to me said he was a musician and had an extensive record collection. I told him about KBOO, and he agreed to do a jazz show that was an excellent and educational program.

Another time, I attended a performance by a local bluegrass band. The group's leader told me he had a thousand bluegrass records. I immediately asked him if he'd do a show. It, too, became another popular and educational music program.

And when anyone well known was in town, I invited him or her to speak or perform live on the air.

I became more aware of the ego trying to be important. Despite it, necessary things continued to happen like living across the street from a library run by the Theosophical Society. The metaphysical books I read were informative, but it wasn't the same as learning directly from Vassily.

It reminded me of another of his tricks: he'd buy books — six or seven at a time — and the day after tell me in detail the subject matter of each one. I once marked a book and would have known if it had been opened. It hadn't been, yet he explained a new technique the author had for growing mushrooms from spores.

There was a growing, diverse music scene in Portland, some

of which could be attributed to the wide-ranging music programs on KBOO. I frequently invited local musicians to play live on the air, which gave me an idea. I talked Roger into letting me produce a benefit concert. The blues, bluegrass, and folk musicians who'd played at the station all agreed to perform.

It was a huge financial success. I knew Roger was happy when he told me he was doubling both our salaries, from "next to nothing" to "close to nothing"!

The chief engineer announced he'd acquired a used thousand-watt transmitter that'd be ready in two weeks, Roger rented a storefront for the new studio, and soon we had more paying sub-scribers than ever before. It had been three years of hard work, and I needed a change.

One evening, Alex, a volunteer, was doing his excellent program "Third-World Music." He was playing something I'd heard before, but I couldn't remember what it was.

"It's from the Andes," Alex said. "Music of the Incas, by a group called Urubamba."

"If the Andes have music like that," I said, "I want to go there!"

And that was the beginning of my new adventure. After retiring from KBOO, it wasn't long before everything began to fall into place.

I'd become friends with Jim, an avid bicycler who built custom bike frames. I'm grateful to him for introducing me to riding and sharing his wisdom on cycling: "If you're going to ride, you have to love hills. Look for the steepest hills you can find and then ride to the top!"

Jim asked if I wanted to build my own bike frame and offered to help me. He also asked if I wanted a job doing silver soldering and brazing at a small fabricating shop where he worked. It was part time, from eight to one, but the pay was good. The hours were perfect, as the local community college was offering a beginning course in Spanish each weekday afternoon, and I wanted to take it.

I used the meditative, hypnotic state called *crepusculum* to learn Spanish. Vassily had shown me how the learning process, combined with imagination, could be enhanced. While in a relaxed, self-hypnotic state, I imagined myself already speaking Spanish. It worked, as I got straight As and the instructor's commendation.

Vassily had visited Portland a couple of times and liked it. A month before my departure, he made the move permanent. He told me my learning was going well, but there was more to come.

My plan was to ride my new bike from Portland to San Bernardino in Southern California and then decide how to continue the trip through Mexico and Central America and on to South America.

I had no idea what route to take on my ensuing trip, or how I'd continue on to South America. In my final talk with Vassily, I asked about a conversation we had regarding decisions.

"Being indecisive," he said, "is a problem only for your lower mind. Set all decision making aside. Doing nothing is still positively doing something, as it's allowing your higher mind to reveal the action you're to take. The rapport with your higher mind will get stronger each time you allow it to assist."

The morning of my departure, in the summer of 1974, a cycling friend gave me a gift: four small pieces of transparent paper better known as windowpane LSD. I put them in a small bottle with a dropper cap and filled it with water. I shook it, put three little squirts in my mouth, climbed on my bike and started riding south. The small amount of spiked water was just enough to free my mind, put a big grin on my face, and open a current of energy. My legs would be pedaling away, seemingly separate from me sitting on my bike enjoying the scenery.

I kept on back roads through the lush Willamette Valley. It was refreshing to see the natural beauty of streams and rivers, the various fruit and nut orchards, and the other farmlands up close. The air was filled with the aromas of wheat, hops, strawberries and peppermint. I rode through Aurora, Woodburn, Salem, and Albany to Corvallis, where I camped that first night on a baseball field. Upon awakening, I took the dropper from the special bottle and, as I did nearly every morning, put three quick squirts in my mouth.

With the snowcapped peaks of the Cascades on my left and the pine tree–covered Coast Range mountains on my right, I continued down the wide valley through Eugene.

While riding, I tried to remain aware. But interfering thoughts continued to come out of nowhere. When they did, I attempted to study and learn where they'd come from. I laughed and wondered, *Will they never end?*

Continuing my ride south through Cottage Grove and Sutherlin, I turned east at Wilbur and rode up into the Cascades, where I stayed at a campground near Toketee Lake.

Early the next morning, I was off again. With the smell of pine trees in the air, riding up in the mountains was smooth and easy. After going east a ways, I turned south and passed Diamond Lake and the larger Crater Lake, which looked just like the pictures I'd seen of it. Then it was through Fort Klamath and along Klamath Lake to the town of Klamath Falls.

It was late afternoon when I stopped at a convenience store to take a break and have a beer. I was opening the can when a truck pulled up and a giant got out. He was well over six feet tall and weighed close to three hundred pounds.

He looked at me and my beer, smiled, stuck out his hand, and said, "Hi, my name's Manley. And man, you got the right idea!"

As we shook hands, I thought, *The name sure fits.* I introduced myself, and he went into the store and was back out a minute later with a six-pack of his own. In our ensuing conversation, he told me he was a student and football player at the University of Nevada, but he was working during the summer helping build a huge water tank. I asked him if he knew where a campground was.

Looking at my bike, Manley said, "I'd sure like to do what you're doin', but I can't find a bike that's big enough. And, hey, you don't have to stay at a campground. The company I work for rented me an apartment, and you can stay there.

"There's an all-you-can-eat buffet just a block away," said the happy giant. Then he laughed and said, "I sure get my money's worth at that place! We can do some serious eatin', have a few beers, and you can tell me more about your bike trip."

Talking to Manley made me realize how grateful I was to be on this adventure. I traced the reason for that feeling all the way back to 1966 and a special day in Golden Gate Park.

Vassily had answered my question on how to reach higher-mind awareness by saying, "The higher mind doesn't contain your everyday, habitual thinking process. That has to be set aside before full awareness and true intelligence can be realized. Being aware of, but not reacting to, those lower-mind thoughts allows your higher mind to see the truth, help solve problems, and guide you."

I compared my LSD experiences to full awareness while falling asleep.

The following morning I rode across the Oregon state line and into Modoc County in California. The road continued through the small town of Tulelake and then into a high-altitude flatland covered with scrub pine trees, sagebrush and a few streams.

I stopped in the little town of Bieber and camped out in their cemetery. It was appropriate as I was dead tired.

The next morning, I took three squirts of windowpane water, packed up, and climbed on my bike. Following my front wheel, I headed south and rode around the base of snowcapped Mount Lassen. I ended up on a back road that led to Chico, some fifty miles farther south. The only place to spend the night was a remote campground with no place to eat.

In the morning I rode toward Chico and the first place that served breakfast. I was hungry and pedaled fast.

I continued on back roads through small towns I'd never heard of before, like Dayton and Glenn. About five miles from Colusa, as the sun set, I ran into a bug barrage. The air was thick with millions of winged insects. It was like a scene from a Hitchcock movie. When I arrived in Colusa, the little pests were all over me. That was the only night on the whole trip that I stayed in a motel. It took two hours to clean the insects off the bike, and me.

From there, I rode south near the Sacramento River, turned west by Lake Berryesa, and then pedaled south through the Napa Valley.

It was hot, and the sweat was dripping off me as I rode alongside a huge grape vineyard. My throat was parched with thirst. Up ahead I spotted an old wooden building that housed a convenience store. A sign in the front window advertised fresh-squeezed lemonade. I went in and ordered a large glass from the smiling young woman who ran the store.

I thanked her and nodded toward a flank of glass doors.

"I see you have a walk-in cooler. Would you mind if I stepped in there for a few minutes?"

"Sure, go ahead," she said, laughing. "Here's a chair. Sit down and relax."

Five minutes later I came out of the cooler completely refreshed. I told her about my journey, the places I'd camped, the insects, and that I was riding to Southern California. From there I planned to continue on to South America.

I asked if she knew of a campground in the area.

"There isn't one," she replied, "but that's OK. You can stay at my house. It's just up the road, in the middle of this vineyard. But you have to do something for me in return: send me a postcard from Peru!"

After a good night's sleep on a couch, in a little house, in the middle of a vineyard, in Napa Valley, I contemplated the young woman who'd requested a thank-you from Peru. She hardly knew me, but she wanted me to succeed.

I recalled that Vassily's tarot card reading had indicated my move to Portland would lead to new, enjoyable opportunities. The radio station, and then bicycling, and now this travel adventure made me wonder if he'd ever been wrong.

Back in the saddle again, I rode down through Marin County to Sausalito. Instead of going over the Golden Gate Bridge, which I'd been on hundreds of times, I crossed the bay to San Francisco on the ferry.

I stayed for three days and again realized the uniqueness of San Francisco. People will come and go, but The City will never change.

Then it was back on the road again, riding south along the coast through Half Moon Bay to Santa Cruz, where I camped out on the University of California campus. That was the first time I'd ridden next to that vast, mystifying body of salt water, the Pacific Ocean.

After squirting three drops of my own mystifying water in my mouth, I continued down Highway 1. It went through Monterey and onto the narrow, winding coast road of Big Sur. With cliffs straight up on my left and straight down to the ocean on my right, it was a breathtaking ride. It was a windy day, and a strong gust nearly blew me off the road and down on the rocks below.

Later that day, I came across a secluded campground. A nearby waterfall provided a pool of water that was ideal for cooling off. After a two-day regenerating stay, it was time to move on.

Leaving the campground, I pedaled hard to get my momentum going. I looked down at the bike — the one I'd built with my own hands — and realized, without a doubt, that this was the most fun I'd ever had in my life!

It was a beautiful ride all the way down the coast. I passed Hearst Castle in San Simeon and rode into Morro Bay. It was dark when I arrived, and I ended up camping out on a golf course. At dawn, I thanked the first foursome for their wake-up call.

The dawn was filled with thick coastal fog. Before starting out, I went to a place with a murky view of Morro Bay.

I hadn't understood the truth in all of the discussions I'd had with Vassily. One thing he'd said, though, was becoming clear: my awareness was constantly being interrupted by intrusive thoughts that I didn't initiate. If I didn't react to the thoughts, but quietly looked at them, they didn't seem to bother me.

My bicycle trek continued south through Pismo Beach, into the high hills to Buellton and Solvang, and then by Lake Cachuma, and downhill into Santa Barbara.

My itinerary included a two-day stay in Isla Vista at the home of some girls who were friends of my brother, Steven. They were students at UC Santa Barbara. Friendly and hospitable, they included me in their plans. The gals were all going to the beach and asked if I wanted to come along. On the way, I learned that this particular beach was for nude sunbathers only.

I'd been riding with my shirt off, so my upper body was tan. I wore bike shorts, so my legs were the same. In between, however, I was as white as the sand on the beach. The outcome was obvious: my butt got so sunburned and blistered that I couldn't sit down. I had to stay an extra night, sleeping on my stomach, in order to be able to get back on my bike. Everyone had a good laugh about it, including me.

I wanted to leave early in order to make it to Long Beach, a ride of 130 miles. I left at sunrise and rode to Santa Barbara and then, by necessity, on the freeway for about twenty miles to Ventura and Oxnard.

It was a beautiful day as I rode down the coast through Malibu and into Santa Monica. All of a sudden, there was congested traffic. I'd arrived in Los Angeles. I rode by Los Angeles International Airport, through Redondo Beach and into Long Beach, arriving in the late afternoon.

Two days later, I rode the final sixty-five miles to my final destination, my mother's home in San Bernardino. She'd been expecting me and was exhilarated that I'd made it.

My 1,500-mile bicycle tour of Oregon and California was completed. I was glad it was over but sad to see it end. I'd enjoyed every single minute of it. I looked back and saw how things had fallen into place on the entire ride: the friendly people I'd met, the places I'd visited, and the freedom of movement my bicycle had given me.

The one thing Vassily taught me that seemed to work was not interfering, but it wasn't easy. It was difficult to be alert and aware, as opinions and thoughts would pop up out of nowhere and hijack my attention.

It was almost time for the next phase of my trip into Mexico and Central America. I had no idea how I'd be traveling, but I was anxious to find out. I was also wondering what metaphysical insights from Vassily would be revealed on the journey.

CHAPTER SIX

*"That which was the beginning of all things under heaven
we may speak of as the Mother of all things."*
— TAO TE CHING

*"The world as a great mother from whose womb
all of life ensued."* — RIANE EISLER

*"The great Mother Goddess, independent of a male
counterpart, flourished in the oldest period
of Babylonian history."* — WIKIPEDIA

"IT WAS nice helping those now-friendly ascenders from Kontrarian," I said. "But before that arguing planet, you were going to tell me about the first worshipping religion on Earth."

"OK, but I'll take a different approach this time. Let's see if you can figure out what happened when the Earthlings asked the inevitable questions: What is this place? Where did it come from? And where did I come from? I'll give you the scenario, and you tell me the answer."

"OK, I'm ready."

"The humans living in the garden paradise had no previous knowledge of what life was about. So what did they experience that so impressed them that it initiated a worshipping religion?"

"I think the answer's in the sky," I said. "They have a sun that appears every day and moves across it. What's the explanation for that?"

"No doubt, they would've wondered."

"And at night the stars with — by the way, Captain, how many moons does Earth have?"

"Just one."

"Their moon gliding across the night sky in its many phases must've amazed them."

"They surely must've noticed," said the Captain.

"I think they were sun and moon worshippers."

"That's a good guess, but not the right one."

"OK, I give up. What was it?"

"It came from the humans themselves, with the birth of their offspring. They were in reverent awe of a mother giving birth as the origin of life. This brought about the worship of a female deity, a goddess, as the mother and source of all life. They also worshipped her as the one who gave birth to Earth and heaven. Everything was provided by the female goddess, giver of all life and the mother of the universe."

"Wow," I said. "Their god was a gal."

"Michael, you never cease to amuse me."

"You mean amaze, don't you?"

"All mothers love their children, so the humans knew the goddess loved them. Because of that adoration, they developed a worshipping religious practice. But it wasn't a female-dominated religion. They saw that mothers gave birth to males and females equally. There was a cooperative equality among them that carried over into all aspects of their lives."

"Wait a sec, Captain. Did this goddess really exist or was she invented?"

"Good question. All cultural groups, through thought, create a concept of their deity."

"I'm going to have to think about that."

"Please do, because you've come across something very important. Worshipping the goddess as the creator brought to a peak everything in the garden paradise. It was a place and time of plenty, where women and men lived in harmony."

There was a profound moment of silence until I asked, "So what happened? Is the religion on Earth today associated with goddess worship?"

"There's a religion that refers to the garden paradise as the place where humans were created. They also claim it's where the downfall of mankind began. They call it the Garden of Eden."

"At least they know it existed."

"Not really," said the Captain. "They don't know the true story, and they have no idea what was really meant by 'the downfall of mankind.'

"I'll continue with the beginning of that downfall after we assist some ascenders. Our new orders are ready."

With a laugh and a snap of his fingers, the orders appeared. "Read it off, Michael. Where're we headed this time?"

"We're going to the coordinates WUT4 and the planet Beecuzz."

"Sure," said the smiling Captain. "I've been there a number of times because Beecuzz has a lot of ascenders!"

CHAPTER SEVEN

"The world is a country which nobody ever yet knew by description; one must travel through it oneself to be acquainted with it."
— LORD CHESTERFIELD

"To travel is to take a journey into yourself." — DENA KAYE

"Where fear is present wisdom cannot be." — LACTANIUS

"Adversity is the first path to truth."
— GEORGE GORDON BYRON

THE bicycle trip was over, and it was time for another plan. I was going to divide the ensuing journey into two parts: initially through Mexico and Central America, taking a break in Costa Rica, and then on to South America on the second leg.

Stopping in Costa Rica was important financially. My plan was to find work there and make enough money to continue on to South America. It seemed plausible, since there were a lot of American retirees, expatriates, and businessmen living there. I didn't know a single person between Tijuana and Tierra del Fuego, but before I'd left Portland the president of the Friends of Costa Rica had given me the name of a Costa Rican doctor to contact. My issue now was how to get there.

While pondering the situation, I recalled Vassily's words. "Don't let your opinions and thoughts determine the outcome of a difficult undertaking. Don't defeat yourself. Know that it's been resolved, and then do what's already been accomplished."

I was glancing through the newspaper want ads and came across a 1962 Chevy panel truck for sale. After a look and a test drive, I knew it was meant to be. The owner accepted my $350, and I drove away in my "new" truck. "This is how I'm goin' to Costa Rica!" I yelled out.

When by myself, I could hear Vassily's voice going over something important: "You have to learn how your own mind works. How decisions are influenced by fear and desire. Be aware of and observe your own mental activity as it happens. Learning how your mind functions will provide insights that will free you from its tyranny."

I was ready to roll, but I decided to look for someone to come along and share expenses. I'd heard about a travel service that matched riders with drivers, so I gave them a call.

"There was a couple in here last week," the voice on the phone said, "but they were looking for a ride to Honduras — wherever that is. You want their number anyway?"

I called and made arrangements to meet Margaret, a smiling, attractive gal, and David, an intelligent guy with a comic wit. They'd just graduated from UC San Diego and were ready for a vacation. David's brother was married to a woman from Honduras, so they'd decided to visit her family. I told them about my plan to take three or four months to get to Costa Rica. They said the leisurely pace was fine with them, too.

Since we'd be camping along the way, a propane stove, cooking utensils, a five-gallon bottle for drinking water, and a large ice chest were collected.

On the day after Christmas of 1974, we departed. As we drove south across the Southern California desert, it hit me: *Hey, I'm on my way to Central America!*

MEXICO

We crossed the border just south of Yuma, Arizona, and drove into the town of San Luis Rio Colorado, Sonora, Mexico. There was no turning back. We'd crossed the proverbial Rubicon.

Northern Mexico is mainly desert, but on our second day we saw a sign with *El Mar* (The Sea) and an arrow pointing off to the right. A map showed we were a half hour from the Mar de Cortés, otherwise known as the Gulf of California. We turned down the road, passed through the dusty village of El Desemboque, and reached the ocean. There were a few dilapidated palm-frond huts on the nearly deserted beach. It would never be on a postcard, but it was our first stop and that made it special.

Vassily had told me, "The mind makes a wonderful servant but a terrible master." I was learning about the disruptions and traps caused by thoughts and opinions. Sometimes I was able to stop them and wonder where in the hell they had come from. But many times they grabbed my attention and wouldn't let go.

It was a cool evening, so we lit a campfire. It must have been the warm glow that attracted a visit from the only person living at the beach. Juan, a poor fisherman, had a bandaged leg and was using a stick of driftwood as a cane.

David and I ran into him in the morning as we strolled down the beach. He asked if we'd help clear his fishing net, as he couldn't because of his injured leg.

Visible due to the low tide was a pole and a long gill net that stretched out in the water. Juan said all we had to do was wade out, lift the net, pull the fish free, and put them in two gunnysacks he gave us. It sounded easy enough.

We headed out in the water to a little over waist deep and lifted up the net. Ensnared were four fish and two small sharks. A little farther out we found four fish and three bigger sharks. We ventured out farther and there were five netted fish and four much larger sharks. The water was infested with sharks, so we headed back to shore.

Back on the beach, David knew but asked Juan anyway: "How'd you hurt your leg?"

"I was clearing my net a few days ago," answered the fisherman with a wry grin, "and a shark bit me."

We drove south through Hermosillo, the Sonoran state capital, and then on to the busy port city of Guaymas. After a short inland detour through Obregon, we arrived at the coast.

For four hundred miles, the main road south ran parallel to the shoreline but inland a ways. It usually took ten minutes, on a side road, to reach the ocean. If there was a nice beach, we'd stay and camp. If not, we'd take another road until we found a good spot.

We visited small towns with colorful central markets to buy groceries. Then it was back to the coast where we'd prepare a meal and dine by the sea. Most of the places we camped were remote and nameless, but they had beautiful beaches, lots of palm trees, rolling ocean waves and a never-before-seen sunset.

After traveling in Mexico for a week, I became aware of being uncomfortable. I felt intimidated in an unfamiliar country where I didn't fully understand the language.

There was a hint of an answer, though, when I remembered a conversation with Vassily during which he'd said, "Any sign of fear is an impediment to being aware and discovering the truth. You need to look at fear without passing judgment on it. By studying your fear, you'll realize it all started with a thought or opinion!" That glimpse was the beginning of a whole new realization for me.

We continued our beach excursions as we traveled farther south. We passed through the small port town of Topolobampo, where the ferry from La Paz docked. The only large town we visited was Mazatlán, where we briefly stayed in a trendy trailer park. But we were spoiled and not interested in where the tourists stayed.

We found a great beach four miles south of San Blas. We camped on a cliff with an artist's panorama of the ocean. A local man informed us that the property we were on was owned by an American, but he wasn't around. There was room for an RV next to a palm-frond structure with a little shower. It lacked hot water, but we used it anyway. Until then, our showers had come from a five-gallon plastic container with a cap that I'd drilled holes in for the shower effect. We'd fill it with water in the morning and let it sit in the sun all day. By evening there was enough warm water for what we called a luxurious shower.

With the arrival of the campsite owner, Margaret, David, and I unanimously voted to hit the road to Tepic and then go farther inland to the congested city of Guadalajara.

Its huge, four-story central market was perfect for restocking supplies. It contained hundreds of individual shops where just about anything could be purchased. There was a colorful produce area, an odiferous meat section, clothing stores, and shops for repairing everything from watches to large appliances.

After a couple of days exploring the streets of the city, we decided it was time to get back to the coast and look for more of those beautiful, peaceful beaches.

Before departing, I looked back at what else Vassily had said about fear. It hadn't been clear to me then, but I was beginning to see how thoughts initiated fear.

"What people psychologically fear," Vassily said, "are incidents that haven't yet happened. They're only ideas, formed by thoughts and opinions. Thought-produced fear is one way the ego maintains its power over us. Freedom from fear takes a great deal of self-study, but it's worth the effort."

I realized that many thoughts that produce psychological fear came from a desire for security. It's why people join groups, become members of a religion, and are nationalistic. But I had a feeling there was more to it.

After leaving Guadalajara, we skirted around large Lake Chapala and ended up back by the ocean at Playa Azul. That was where two first-time encounters took place.

The first happened ten minutes after our arrival. I headed straight for the cool ocean water, but lying on the sandy ocean floor was an unassuming stingray. When I stepped on it, the tail, with a sharp barb on the end, whipped back and stung me on the top of my foot. I felt the pain all day.

The second encounter took place a week later as we were leaving. It was a roadblock manned by the Mexican army. It was the first, but not the last, we encountered while driving south along the coast. Apparently they'd been set up to subdue antigovernment activity and marijuana smuggling.

The soldiers demanded to see everything in the back of the truck. It took over an hour to get everything out and, after they'd seen that we didn't have any pot or guns, back in.

Before leaving California, I'd visited a used-book store looking for maps and information on Central America. They were throwing out a stack of old *Playboy* magazines because the centerfolds were missing. One contained an interview with John Lennon, so I took it and ten others with interesting articles. I put them under the seat in the truck for later reading.

When we arrived at another roadblock, I grabbed a *Playboy* and tossed it by the door in the back.

Three soldiers ordered me to open the truck so they could do a search. They immediately saw the *Playboy* and picked it up. I smiled and said they could keep it. Suddenly they were no longer interested in the truck's contents! I casually got back in the truck and drove off. This time, it only took a minute. I'll thank Hugh Hefner for his assistance next time I see him.

The incident provided another insight, as it reminded me of the Spaceman game Vassily had taught me. He'd used it to get me to see the importance of being awake and aware, but it'd also allowed me to see some of the funny things people do.

I'd been laughing more, but who wouldn't? My only care was *Where's another beach?* I thought about it and blamed Vassily for the hilarity. I'm sure he would have laughed right along with me at the accusation.

We continued our southerly course to laid-back Zihuatanejo and camped out on its superb horseshoe bay for a week. The days were extremely hot, so we spent a lot of time in the cool water.

The day we left was another scorcher, so David got some beer and ice for the drive. It kept us cool as we cruised down the hardly traveled road. It also helped when we came to a wide river with a washed-out bridge. In its place were narrow planks of wood, laid out inches above the flowing water. One slip and we'd be in the drink.

After a big gulp of beer, I smiled at the annoying attempt of thoughts to invoke fear and recalled what Vassily had said: "Don't allow speculative thoughts to determine the outcome."

I put the ol' truck in gear and drove straight to the other side. David and Margaret cheered, and we happily continued on to famous Acapulco.

We camped a few miles north of the tourist trap at Pie de la Cuesta. It had the strangest surf I'd ever seen. Waves broke on a sloped beach and then retreated without the usual flow up on the sand. It was either stand on dry sand, in the middle of a huge wave or beyond it, where the water was too deep to touch bottom. Body surfing was out.

After a quiet week, we drove south to a small campground at

Lagunas de Chacahua National Park. We were the only campers and soon discovered why. Just after dark the air grew thick with mosquitoes. Sleeping was impossible. With a thin sheet it was still unbearably hot, but removing the cover brought on a ceaseless attack from the bloodsuckers. We hastily departed long before the sun came up.

We drove two hours south to Puerto Escondido. It had a nice beach but was more crowded than the idyllic spots we'd become used to.

We moved a little farther south to Puerto Angel and a campsite just outside of town. It was in the middle of a shady coconut grove and next to another tranquil beach.

That evening I told my companions about a couple I'd met at a party back in Portland. As I recalled, John and Jane were moving to Puerto Angel. I found their rustic house in a canyon above town. We spent several fun nights with them, drinking John's homemade fermented pineapple juice.

Visiting these folks made me ponder the past and how deep and ingrained memories are in our minds. I laughed as it became clear to me: people remember the past, but the past doesn't remember them!

We left Puerto Angel and drove through the mountains to Oaxaca. It was a big city, but I liked it. The *zócalo*, or main central plaza, was the best I'd seen. It had a bandstand with nightly musical performances. Facing it, on all sides, were numerous shops, restaurants, and bars.

We learned about the local Zapotec Indian culture by visiting their ruins at Monte Alban and Mitla. I figured the invading Spaniards had converted them but discovered they still used one of the most widely spoken Native American languages.

At the huge, human-bumper-car-style Sunday market on the streets in the center of town, we met Kathleen from California and her boyfriend Andreas from Norway. They'd been traveling and camping in a Volkswagen bus.

We decided to caravan together farther south to San Cristóbal de las Casas in the state of Chiapas. We made one stop on the way, at Tehuantepec. Margaret and Kathleen wanted to see the strange town where females ruled — a matriarchal society. The women were running the shops and doing all the work while the men sat around talking to each other. David, Andreas and I agreed that the Tehuantepec lifestyle looked good to us.

In San Cristóbal, Kathleen met an American woman who was living there. When asked about a campsite, she replied, "Would you like to rent a house for a hundred and fifty dollars a month?" She pointed to a structure visible on a hill overlooking the town. The American builder-owner was being detained in the local jail and needed the money.

It was a rustic, two-story house built of large rocks and cement with rough wooden floors. The house had no electricity or running water, but there was a well close by. The best part was its huge deck with a beautiful view of the whole valley and town down below. Everyone wanted to rent it, and that was fine with me. We were getting claustrophobic in the truck and needed a break.

Everybody was content sitting on the deck, sipping beer and taking in the view. I, on the other hand, was the adventurous one. We were in the northern Mayan Indian region, and I wanted to see some of it.

My first solo outing was to a Sunday festival in the small village of Tenejapa. Most of the attendees were indigenous Indians wearing their native attire of white muslin with a red sash or belt. It was a small and extremely poor village with dusty dirt roads, so the celebration was meager.

I'd seen a lot of poverty in Mexico, and there was bound to be more in other countries. I tempered my feelings with another

Vassilyism: "Never feel sorry for someone in an adverse situation. It provides them with an opportunity to learn. In fact, adversity is the best teacher of life, as it forces them to ask, 'What's it all about and why?' They actively seek answers and are, therefore, open to learning the truth. It's the people without adversity you should feel sorry for, as they're never forced to seek the truth."

On my second excursion, I wanted to go to Palenque for two reasons: to see the great Mayan ruins and to try the magic mushrooms, which I'd heard were the best.

There was a problem, though. It was seventy miles — as the crow flies — to Palenque, and there were no direct roads. One was being built, but it was far from completion. I made a different plan, but I wasn't sure if it was possible.

I recalled the long walks Vassily and I had set out on, not knowing where we were going or why, and he'd say, "Turn your thinking off and let your higher mind guide you. You'll be shown the way, and you'll end up right where you're supposed to be."

I started out taking a bus thirty miles to the village of Ocosingo. From there, I waded across a river and hiked over rolling hills and through a tropical jungle, all on trails with no signs. There was never a doubt about which way to go, as every path was the right one. There was a drawback, though: I had water but little food. It was nearly dark when I arrived at the camp of the road builders, who were kind enough to let me eat with the workers.

When I asked about a place to sleep, they said I could stay in a small shack that would keep out the snakes, scorpions and insects. Taking a peek inside, I discovered it was where my hosts stored their dynamite. It didn't matter to me. I slept soundly on a bed of six boxes of dynamite.

A company truck gave me a ride to Agua Azul, which was halfway to Palenque. It was an unusual place: millions of gallons of crystal-clear water gushed out of the ground, forming pool after pool for a mile. The pools were connected by small waterfalls, so one could go unimpeded, by diving and swimming, to each successive pool.

Daily, a dilapidated bus sputtered its way to Agua Azul, and I rode it on its fifteen-mile return trip to Palenque. A campground two miles out of town provided a convenient place to stay; it was within walking distance to the ruins. The twenty or so fellow campers appeared to be there for the same two reasons I was.

The ruins were impressive. The tall pyramid Templo de las Inscripciones contained the crypt of Palenque's greatest ruler, King Pacal, who was buried in 683 CE. After climbing to the top of it, one could pass through a small door and go deep down inside the structure on a narrow stairway to the burial area. Carved on a huge thick slab of stone covering the sarcophagus was an image of the king. He was seated in a reclined position in what appeared to be the interior of a rocket ship. Flames shot out from the bottom where rockets would have been located. It made me ponder the possibilities.

It was time for my other reason for visiting Palenque: the notorious magic mushroom! Tim, a fellow psychedelic fancier, and I went mushroom hunting just after sunrise. We were in a cow pasture with knee-high grass when Tim found one. It was the most beautiful mushroom I'd ever seen: about four inches in diameter with a superb golden dome.

We rinsed it off, broke it evenly, and each devoured a half — right there on the spot. We walked to the next field, which was flat and had a treelined stream beside it. In no time it happened: I was stoned to the hilt, thoroughly overwhelmed by the amazing effects. In expanding wonder, my mind was opened to a clear insight into the ludicrous ways of the world. I saw that humans had lost the connection to learning and higher-mind intelligence and were now stuck in the mental quagmire of everyday life. Along with the realization came a release that was as close to total freedom as I'd ever experienced. It was the best trip I'd ever taken.

Tim also understood what was happening. As we were discussing our experiences, the laughter burst forth. For several hours, anything we said or did prolonged the hilarity. I laughed so hard my facial muscles hurt and my stomach felt like it had been turned inside out. The best description of that day: a physical, mental and spiritual cleansing.

After we'd had a funny conversation about the absurdities of mundane life, Vassily had come up with the idea of laughing oneself to freedom. "If people could see the hilarious things they do in so-called normal life and were able to laugh at them, it just might lead to psychological freedom. How interesting. Just see the comedy in everyday existence, and laugh yourself to nirvana!"

That was the first time since leaving California that I'd gone anywhere alone. It revealed the advantages that uncompromised travel and existence provided.

Vassily told me that metaphysical learning must be done alone. "I'm actually not your teacher," he said. "We're just discussing possibilities that you'll have to fully realize on your own. Nobody can do it for you."

A few days later, I caught a ride on the long, indirect route back to San Cristóbal.

With the month-long stay at the house over, it was time for David, Margaret and I to hit the road. That was fine with me, as Central America was waiting just down the highway.

GUATEMALA

The second country on our trip gradually took on a different appearance. It was noticeable in the first place we stopped. The town of Huehuetenango was in a pine forest in the mountains, and that meant the climate was cooler.

While sitting in the central plaza, contemplating the goose bumps on my arms, I noticed a radio station across the street. I was soon inside introducing myself as a fellow radio person. The friendly staff gave me a tour and asked me to record an ID announcement in English. I tuned in to the station and heard it as we were driving out of town. Margaret thought it was cool.

Quetzaltenango was also located in the higher elevation mountains. Intrigued with the names of the towns, I asked a local lady to interpret. She told me the colorful quetzal was the national bird of Guatemala, but it was on the endangered species list. A picture of one was on their paper money, which were called quetzales. It was a golden, green and scarlet bird with tail feathers three feet long.

As for Quetzaltenango, it was a quiet town. The final night we camped up on the side of a nearby volcano at Fuentes Georginas hot springs. In the cool evening air, the hot-water pools felt good.

A couple hours down the road, we stopped at picturesque Lago de Atitlán. A ring of mountains, which included three big volcanoes, surrounded the huge lake. Panajachel, the small town on the water's edge, had an artsy air to it.

Early one morning we went to the extraordinary Indian market at Chichicastenango. It was a lively scene. The Mayans were all dressed in distinctive homespun clothing with the symbols and colors that were particular to their home village. Tourism had begun to affect the town, with the sale of trinkets and garments to outsiders. Even so, the heart of the market hadn't changed much for the Mayans: they were there to purchase commodities to cart home. It was a colorful site.

I went on two excursions by myself: one to the Indian market in Santiago, a Mayan village on the far side of the lake, and the other to the old Guatemalan capital.

Antigua Guatemala was a beautiful old city with colonial-style buildings and cobblestone streets. It was one of the first foreign communities in the Americas and the original capital. I'd chosen the wrong day to visit, though. It was Easter and the place was mobbed with church folks. The multitudes were there for a religious procession through the narrow streets. I saw very few traditionally attired Mayan Indians at the event.

I was beginning to realize how fear manipulated my life. It was usually forced into my attention by a thought or opinion. It was important to question and study each thought in order to learn that it was the initiator of the fear. I recalled one of Vassily's basic teachings: "The best way to learn the truth is to question everything. Not only in the outside world, but everything about yourself as well, meaning your thoughts and the actions that result from them. By questioning, your mind will be open and ready to receive an answer."

All main roads lead to the country's new capital, Guatemala City. In "Guat City" we went to the Hippodromo for the hilarious Guatemalan-style horse races. Any kind of horse was eligible to run, and there were many of those "any kinds" on the track. I bet on one race and actually won about a dollar.

After visiting the chaotic central market, the university, several museums and some good restaurants, we decided to head farther south.

EL SALVADOR

Since we had to pass through El Salvador to get to Honduras anyway, we chose the coast road. We were hoping to find some beaches like those in Mexico, but we were disappointed. But this was another country I'd never been in before, and that made it a new adventure.

For example, the port city of La Libertad didn't have much to offer, but wafting through the air was a mouthwatering aroma that led me to a great outdoor restaurant and my first *pupusa*. They're the delicious Salvadoran corn tortilla specialty stuffed with sausage and cheese.

We drove inland to the capital, San Salvador, which was a crowded city. In fact, the whole country was overpopulated: we decided to relieve some of the problem by departing. Besides, we'd been on the road for nearly five months, and David thought it about time he got to his relatives' house in Honduras.

HONDURAS

At the Honduran border we encountered an attempt to extract a five-dollar under-the-table payment for permission to enter the country. We told the border guard we wanted a valid receipt and would seek a refund when we reached the capital of Tegucigalpa. A bit startled, the guard said that since we were tourists, this time the fee would be waived. It reminded me of the game of liar's poker.

It was almost dark when we arrived at the home of Tía Telma, David's aunt by marriage. She was a very nice lady and made us feel right at home.

Tegucigalpa was a tranquil city to say the least. We did take a three-day excursion, some forty miles on a bumpy, dusty road, to visit other relatives; after a couple of days in that dead-quiet little village, I was ready to return to the much livelier capital.

My money stash was getting low, so I made plans to move on to Costa Rica. David and Margaret decided to go along. They'd stay a week and then return to Aunt Telma's by bus.

NICARAGUA

After crossing into Nicaragua, it was an uneventful drive to the capital of Managua. We continued south, passing the enormous Lago de Nicaragua, a freshwater lake containing man-eating sharks that got there by swimming up a river from the coast. We were warned not to take a dip, even if it was a hot day and the water looked inviting.

COSTA RICA

Our entrance at the Costa Rican border was unusual. The border guards were honest and efficient — two qualities lacking in officials we'd previously encountered.

Having heard glowing reports about the beaches in Costa Rica, we succumbed to the first temptation. Fifty miles into the country, we turned off and headed for the Pacific Ocean and the aptly named Coco Beach. It had beautiful white sand, an abundant supply of coconut trees, and an ideal little bay. The locals were friendly and treated me to some of their delicious homemade lobster ceviche.

After an enjoyable week at Coco, we headed for San José, the capital of the sixth country on our trip.

My self-study on how fear came about also continued while we traveled along. It wasn't surprising, though, as I recalled Vassily saying, "The controlling power of your psychologically conditioned thoughts goes with you everywhere."

In San José I found a great place to park the truck and camp. Behind a big house converted to an Italian restaurant was a sprawling backyard that the owner let a few campers use for a small fee. The Italian proprietor, who always wore a white apron, was a friendly guy.

David and Margaret stayed a couple of days and then departed on their return journey north. I was now completely on my own.

Vassily had told me that signs on the path of life were there to guide one in the right direction. He'd said, "To see or sense them, you have to be aware, as they sometimes appear in subtle ways."

I was sitting in the shade beside my truck, wondering what was next when the owner came running out.

"He's coming! He's coming!" he shouted.

"Who's coming?" I asked.

"*El Presidente!* He comes here once a week for lunch. He loves my cooking."

Just then a big white car pulled into the backyard. Daniel Oduber, the president of Costa Rica, got out and looked over at me. I stood up, smiled and — as kind of a joke, but out of respect too — saluted the president. With a big grin, he returned the gesture.

That not-so-subtle sign gave me some reassurance. I was still concerned, however, about how to make some money and continue on to South America. I didn't know anybody in the country, but I had received a ceremonious greeting from the president, and I had the name of the doctor given to me in Portland by the Friends of Costa Rica.

While trying to sort out my predicament, this insight came to me: thoughts of uncertainty and concern were just another subtle form of fear. Vassily was right. In their devious way, they were trying to influence my freedom. I had to laugh, as I'm devious, too.

I had a problem finding the doctor's name in the phone book. As it turned out, he was a dentist, not a physician. I called, told him who'd given me his name, and made an appointment to meet him that afternoon. It would be difficult to find a nicer person than Ronaldo.

After a cordial exchange, he told me about a man from Oregon who was the new principal of one of the American schools.

"His name is Joe, and here's his phone number."

Ronaldo also informed me that as a Navy veteran, I could go to the Universidad de Costa Rica to study Spanish and receive GI Bill benefits.

"Your timing is good, too," he stated. "Classes start in a week, and I can make arrangements for you to register."

"Thank you," I said wholeheartedly.

Later that day, I called Joe and was invited to his house for coffee. He said his degree was in anthropology. I'd taken some enjoyable classes on the subject, so we had an instant rapport.

A half hour into our conversation, Joe said, "Our school year is about to start, and we need a part-time physical education instructor."

"Gee, phys ed was my minor in college!" I said, stretching the truth.

The hours were from eight until noon, five days a week. My job was to make sure the students got some exercise in the big open field beside the school.

I recalled asking Vassily to tell me more about fear. He'd said, "Life is rampant with subjective fear. It's in society to keep people in line, and government and religion use it to stay in power. Once you realize how they initiate and affect your thought process, you can begin to free yourself."

I'd heard two Americans were opening a bar and grill nearby. I walked over to the location and introduced myself to Lee and Richard. They were in the process of opening a funky place called La Fanega. It would be the only bar in town that sold pitchers of draft beer and the only restaurant that sold quarter-pound hamburgers exactly the same as McDonald's.

During the conversation, we struck a deal. I needed a place to stay, and they needed transportation to get supplies. They had a house with a spare room, and I had a truck.

La Fanega became a hip place for expats and Costa Ricans. Whether it was for the weekend live music or just a place to hang out, it was popular. I'd often help with the bartending.

It was also where I met some interesting people.

Woody had recently graduated from Duke University and inherited some money. His intention was to buy a farm, but confronted with governmental bureaucracy, he never became a farmer.

Mark's family had started the famous Tupperware company. After tiring of government infringement in their business affairs, they sold it and moved to Costa Rica.

There were also two business ventures I entered into with people I met at La Fanega.

Max, a Costa Rican engineer, worked for an international electronics company. At night he'd built an FM radio transmitter. He installed it at a friend's house up in the mountains just outside of San José. The station broadcast only long-playing music tapes and had no live announcers.

I told Max I'd worked at a radio station, and he flipped out. He asked me to please do a music show. Any money we'd get from commercials would be split fifty-fifty.

I didn't have any albums or tapes, but Woody had brought his entire music collection with him, and he'd surely let me use it. That was how I got involved with *"Cientodos coma tres, Frequencia Modulada, Circuito Estereo, desde la montaña!"*

Fred, an expat American, proposed another business opportunity. I met him one afternoon at La Fanega. We discussed his hobby of analyzing handwriting and how it revealed personality traits. He looked at a sample of mine, laughed, and said, "OK. We can be friends now!"

Fred's business, Bolsa Numismatica, bought gold and silver jewelry and coins. He'd offer 40 percent below their value in immediate cash, and he had lots of takers. He'd sell them back in the United States at the spot price, ensuring a 40 percent profit. He sometimes paid more for coins with numismatic value.

I asked him why he didn't sell his purchases here in Costa Rica. Fred admitted he was a lousy salesman.

"Why not let me sell 'em?" I proposed.

"Sure, go ahead. We can split the difference. I'll still make money, and you can make some, too!"

I reflected on what had brought me to this place, at this time. In 1966, if someone had told me that because of taking LSD in Golden Gate Park, I'd be in Costa Rica working to make enough money to continue on a travel adventure to South America, I'd have said they were crazy. But "shut my mouth and open my mind," it was true!

That phrase reminds me of the time Vassily had me read a book by an Indian guru. He wrote about a technique called *japa*, which he claimed stopped habitual thought by repeating an inspirational mantra over and over. After trying it for a few days, I told Vassily it helped some, but when I stopped, the thoughts came back same as before.

"Now you see," he said, "that repeating a mantra doesn't silence habitual, compulsive thoughts. It only exercises them."

Two nights a week, I'd broadcast my radio show. It must've been popular, as the English-language newspaper *Tico Times* did an article about the station with a photo of me at the mic.

My dealings with Fred were profitable, too. Most of my customers were American expats buying jewelry for themselves, their wives, or their Costa Rican girlfriends. I also sold silver and gold coins to people who wanted them for investment.

At the American school, some students wanted me to coach their girls' softball team. After practicing for three weeks, they wanted to play another team. Through a friend at the university, I arranged a game against their older girls' softball squad. The fact they might be overmatched never entered my mind, nor theirs. I just coached, knowing my team would win. And they did, seven to four. There was a write-up in the *Tico Times*, and it was the highlight of my coaching career.

Vassily had suggested I be careful talking about my metaphysical learning with anyone: "Most people are unable to discuss fear. When they hear how it affects their lives, they'll deny it applies to them. They refute it because they've never studied their own thoughts. They've never seen how they initiate fear. In fact, they're unaware of the entire mental process."

During breaks from school, I went on two excursions. One was to the beautiful Tamarindo beach with a girl I'd met in my Spanish class. We enjoyed splashing around in the waves, sitting under palm trees, and watching the beautiful sunsets.

On the second, I went to the east-coast city of Puerto Limón. It included their Caribbean-style Mardi Gras Carnaval, with music, dancing in the streets, a colorful parade and delicious food. The weekend party was nonstop fun.

To recuperate from the festivities, I went thirty miles south of Limón to Cahuita. It's a national park with a coral reef and the best beaches in Costa Rica. There was a popular black-sand beach on one side, but I shared the other sparkling, long, white-sand beach with just two other people.

A travel adventure had been my original reason for this trip, but it had become a transforming lesson, too. I was going over what Vassily had said about fear when a question came up. If psychologically conditioned thoughts were the cause of the fear that kept freedom from being experienced, what other problems did thoughts initiate? I'd soon discover the answers to that question.

The plan had worked: I'd been able to make enough money to get me to South America. A week before leaving I sold the ol' panel truck for exactly what I'd paid for it a year and a half earlier: $350.

It was time and I was excited, because I was goin' to South America!

CHAPTER EIGHT

"Macho barbarians from Europe and Asia came down from the hills bringing a new culture of violence and domination."
— RIANE EISLER

"The world is imprisoned by its own activity."
— HINDU TEACHING

"It is slavery to live in the mind."
— KAHLIL GIBRAN

"I LIKE the planet Beecuzz because it has a lot of ascenders. But will I like what happened to the goddess-worshipping Earthlings?"

"Let's find out," said the Captain. "First, the garden paradise experienced some climate changes. Extremely dry weather slowly caused the land to become arid and uninhabitable. In small groups, the Earthlings moved north to an area called Europe and to the Middle East and South Asia. They adapted to the new land and continued to live in harmony.

"But out beyond them were a number of large nomadic groups from the northern part of Eastern Europe and Northern Asia. They were dramatically opposite to the goddess-worshipping humans. The nomads had a merciless male god, male priests who saw that everyone was subservient, and violent male warriors to carry out conquests.

"The conquering bands moved south and west and began to overthrow the goddess-worshipping groups and impose their ideologies and ways of life on them.

"The most notable change was that the nomads' callous male god replaced the loving female goddess. Rather than dispose of the goddess, they demoted her to follower and supporter. They did that to show that women were now subservient to male authority. Their belief in birth, life, and cooperation was transformed into the invaders' ethos — that power and might ruled. One at a time, the peaceful groups were overtaken and forced to accept the conquerors' lifestyle."

"Captain," I interrupted, "these are two groups with opposite psychological conditioning. What happened with that?"

"The psychological transformation was induced mainly by fear. Ridicule, confinement, torture, and public execution frightened the conquered into subservience. And that began the replacement of the psychological conditioning of the peaceful goddess-worshipping Earthlings with the conditioning of the violent war-god culture."

"I guess it's safe to assume," I said sarcastically, "that the invaders never enjoyed the mushrooms that were available back in the garden paradise."

"No, Michael," the Captain said, "they never had that opportunity. If they had, things might have been different."

"Were the goddess worshippers able to record and save anything about their beliefs?"

"Stories of the garden paradise and goddess religion were told, and some were written down. But most of those accounts were revised by male priests and historians so they conformed to the male-god, authoritarian beliefs. An example is the tale of the Garden of Eden, which was distorted to give a male authoritarian perspective."

"What a story! And that brings up the question again: Did this violent war god really exist, or did they think him up and invent him, too?"

"Again, all the cultures on Earth, through thought, create their own concept of a deity for their particular religion."

"I understand what you're saying, but that brings up the big question: Is there a true god for all Earthlings?"

"There is," said the Captain. "But that real god is infinite and, therefore, outside the humans' restrictive and conditioned thought, which is finite. Most Earthlings are completely unaware of its existence. That infinite god is, in fact, where the ascenders we assist return to."

"I'm starting to get it," I said.

"Eventually you'll understand everything."

"That's easy for you to say. Anyway, if those war-god invaders are related to the present-day Earthlings, I'm gonna predict that life on planet Earth isn't so free and easy!"

"We'll investigate your assumption right after our next assignment."

The Captain let out his unique laugh and snapped his fingers, and new orders were in his hand.

"We're to assist a group of beings who were stuck in a moment of time but are now ready to ascend back to reality. They're at the coordinates BE4 on the planet Andafter."

CHAPTER NINE

"My favorite thing is to go where I've never been."
— DIANE ARBUS

"Certainly, travel is more than seeing the sights; it is a
change that goes on, deep and permanent, in the ideas of living."
— MIRIAM BEARD

"We do not see what is happening, when we are
engaged in the activity of thinking."
— DAVID BOHM, quantum physicist

"Only two things are infinite: the universe and human stupidity;
and I'm not sure about the universe."
— ALBERT EINSTEIN

I BOARDED the bus and sat down at a window seat. Pleasant memories of Costa Rica lingered for a moment but were quickly set aside because I was on my way to South America!

PANAMA

Looking out the window as we motored down the Pan-American Highway, I saw an all-new-to-me countryside. We drove through an upland hilly region and then down to a lowland area with large pastures. We also passed a thick tropical jungle that threatened to grow out and onto the road.

Even though it was a bus, I accepted being chauffeured as a

luxurious indulgence. It also gave me a relaxed opportunity to go over what I'd learned so far.

Vassily had opened the door. I was amazed to discover how simple thoughts initiated and camouflaged fear. The whole process was astounding. I'd never suspected that fear had anything to do with my life. I'd soon learn that thoughts also caused other freedom-restricting problems.

It was midnight when we arrived in the capital. The following week I explored Panama City, mostly on foot. Walking helped me get the feel of a new place. It was nothing for me to walk five or ten miles a day. I could visit all the shops, talk to people, and search for anything unusual.

On my first walkabout, I sensed something new. I was standing on a corner, wondering which way to go, when the perception of being completely alone came over me. I was traveling by myself and loved it! That realization was my initiation as a true traveler, and it was profound. A traveler leaves ordinary life behind — it no longer has attraction or meaning. For an authentic traveler, a new life is created every day.

Early one morning I took the train east across Panama to Colón on the Caribbean coast. The rail line cut a path through the thick jungle alongside the Panama Canal. As seen from the train, huge ships appeared to be landlocked, but were actually floating in the narrow canal or one of its tributaries.

I searched for the best way to get from Panama to Colombia. The area between the two countries, called the Darien Gap, was swampland; there were no feasible roads through it. Wanting to go down the west coast of South America along the Andes, I looked for a flight to western Colombia. Three airlines flew to the city of Cali. I picked the one with the lowest fare: twenty-six bucks one way.

Not having a lot of money, and wanting this trip to last as long as possible, I nearly always chose the lowest-priced transportation, accommodations, and places to eat. The inexpensive transportation was the same the locals traveled on, and there were a myriad of low-cost accommodations. Whether it was a regular hotel or a smaller *pension, hospedaje,* or *hostál,* it was easy to find lodging that was clean, run by a friendly family, and costing around five dollars a night or less.

As for meals, I looked for places where the locals ate. They knew where to get the best food at the best price. Or I went to the food stalls in the central market. The meals they served were always inexpensive and made from fresh ingredients.

The flight to Cali left in the afternoon, so I took the slow, local bus twenty miles out to Tocumen Airport. It was full of cheerful Panamanians who let the driver know I wanted off at the airport. I thanked them, waved good-bye and began walking down the long road to the terminal.

Shuffling along in a country where I'd never been before was similar to the Spaceman game Vassily had taught me. He'd said, "Looking at everything as an outsider of society and the planet will give you insights into people and life. You can then apply what you've learned to yourself. You'll be amazed at how unaware you are of the things you do."

While checking in for the flight, I met three guys from Austria. They had a VW van and were driving to South America. Being unable to cross the Darien Gap, they shipped their VW by boat to the Colombian port of Buenaventura. We'd be flying together to Cali; in a few days they'd go to the port and reclaim their vehicle. We were swapping stories about our travels when they asked if I knew of a place to stay in Cali, preferably inexpensive. I'd bought a used copy of the *South American Handbook*, and this was my first opportunity to use it. I looked up accommodations in Cali and went down the list to a place they should like. It was called Pension Vienna.

They cheered their approval. When I told them it was only three dollars a night, they cheered louder.

After boarding the plane, I found out why the ticket was inexpensive. It took a couple tries to find a seat with a functioning lap belt. It was a bumpy flight, but we made it. I exited the plane, went down the stairs, and stepped onto South America!

COLOMBIA

I stayed a couple nights in Cali. My Austrian friends and I visited a museum and an old church and found a great bakery. On the third day I hopped on a bus for the three-hour ride to Popoyan.

While realizing the positive aspects of traveling alone, I wasn't bothered by being with other travelers for short stints. It mattered not to me — alone or with others, I was going anyway.

Another concept Vassily discussed with me included these words: "As a man thinketh, so shall it be. Through your thoughts, you are a law unto yourself. And that's why it's so important to pay attention to all your thoughts and watch what transpires because of them."

This part of the northern Andes wasn't flat, but it was still conducive to farming. The main crops growing on the steep slopes were coffee and coca. Cups of sweetened coffee and coca tea were the main eye-opening beverages offered by vendors.

Located in a verdant valley, Popoyan was more than 450 years old. The Spanish influence was clearly visible in its architecture. There was a large cathedral on the main plaza and three more churches nearby; all were surrounded by flat-roofed, whitewashed homes.

At the bus station I purchased a ticket to Pasto. I chose the longer, inexpensive route instead of the speedier direct express. The bus took a roundabout circuit that wound up into the Andes and provided spectacular mountain scenery.

When we arrived I didn't feel well. Not sick, but light-headed with no energy. It was probably because Pasto is eight thousand feet above sea level.

Needing to get acclimated for continued travel in the Andes, I used a technique Vassily had shown me to get a mental and physical boost. He'd said there's an energy flow that one can tap into. One need only stand in the star position: facing north, feet spread apart, arms straight out from your sides with fingers of left hand pointing up and fingers of right hand pointing down. It doesn't take long before the subtle energy can be felt flowing in through the left fingers and out through the right. The flow could be boosted by repeating, "I am one with universal life energy. It is flowing through me now. I feel it." It wasn't long before I was reenergized and ready for the next country.

ECUADOR

I'd heard that the main industry at this particular national border crossing was petty smuggling. I went to the Colombian guard station and got my passport stamped. I looked for its counterpart on the Ecuadorian side, but nothing was there. I had to go a mile into the border town of Tulcán, where the immigration office was located, to get a visa. It sure made the local contraband trade easier.

I could tell immediately that I was in another country. Some people lump all of Latin America into one category, but each nation is unique. Some of the differences were obvious. The terrain and climate changed; homes and buildings looked different; there were different makes of automobiles; the ingredients were the same, but the food tasted different; there were spoken accent and slang variations; and clothing styles were distinct. In fact, locals could tell who were foreigners by the shoes they wore.

Perhaps it was traveling solo, the changing cultural backdrop, the dizzying altitude of Andes Mountains, or a combination of all three, but something Vassily told me came to mind: "It's impossible to think and see at the same time. If thought is taking place, there's no visual awareness. By truly seeing, without allowing thought to interfere with an opinion, judgment or description, one becomes awake and aware."

I looked forward to visiting Ibarra, another old colonial town. I stayed a week and took two interesting excursions.

The first was a hike out of town and up into the mountains. I left early in the morning and walked about ten miles, all uphill, on a winding narrow road. Along the way I passed homes with women sitting out front, needle and thread in hand, doing embroidery work. Clothing and other items with intricate needlework designs were offered for sale.

My second outing was to the Indian market in the small town of Otavalo. It's known for indigenous weavings and knit clothing. From a friendly woman, I bought a sweater that buttoned up the front and had side pockets. It kept me warm, and I liked it a lot.

From Ibarra, it was a three-hour bus ride to the capital city of Quito. On the way, another great wonder took place. We passed through the geographical line for which Ecuador was named. For me, it was another momentous occasion: I had crossed the equator and entered the planet's southern hemisphere. I said with a laugh, "It's all downhill from here!"

Quito is located in a valley near the volcano Pichincha. It's divided into new city and old city. Getting around in the old section was confusing, and I sometimes had trouble getting my bearings. The only landmarks on the narrow cobbled streets that went up, down, and around the hills were four-hundred-year-old churches. I was forever wondering where I was. It prompted me to come up with a saying I've used ever since: "I may not know where I am, but

I'm never lost."

The situation reminded me of the time Vassily conveyed an eye-opening point to me. We were quietly strolling down a street we'd never been on before. At the corner he asked me what I'd seen in the previous block.

I hesitated and then said haltingly, "Some shops and a few people."

"Which store had a pink door? What was in the flower-shop window? Who was getting out of the blue car?" he asked.

"I didn't notice," I said truthfully.

"And why was that?"

"I must have been thinking about something."

He looked at me and smiled. Without saying another word, his point was made. That blinded-by-thought lesson made a believer out of me!

After Quito I was anxious to visit Baños, a small resort town. The four-hour bus ride was not comfortable, but there was a great view of the huge, snowcapped volcano Cotopaxi.

Baños means "baths" in English, and in this town it meant thermal baths fed by natural hot springs. When I asked which was the hottest, everyone said, "Baños de la Virgen." From the heated outdoor pools, there was a magnificent view of the source of the water, the volcano Tungurahua. It was a great place to relax and soak, but after a week, I was waterlogged.

Continuing south, I made a stop in the middle of the country. The provincial capital of Riobamba is the geographical center of Ecuador.

The trip provided a stunning view of the Andes, which was now a continuous string of snowcapped mountains. One of them was the unmatched Chimborazo, which is technically the highest mountain in the world. Due to the bulging of the Earth at the equator, its peak is farther from the center of the planet than any other mountain.

My stay in the middle of Ecuador was not long. Eager to go where I'd planned on going all along, the next country to the south overtook me.

I left Riobamba at five in the morning for Huaquillas, the small Ecuadorian border town. After hearing about difficulties crossing into Peru there, I wanted to arrive early.

I was standing at the Ecuadorian border station trying to figure out how to get into Peru. The Peruvian border station was four miles down the road in the town of Tumbes. The only way was to take a small bus into town, get in the long line for a visa, and then get onto a bigger bus going south.

As mentioned earlier, Vassily had advised me to watch for signs to use as a guide. "They appear in many different forms, so you have to be alert," he'd said. I had to laugh, though, as another not-so-subtle sign appeared right in front of me. Across the street were my Austrian friends in their VW van.

We greeted each other, and I asked about a ride across the border with them. It was fast and hassle-free to enter Peru in a private vehicle. They agreed and said they'd even take me all the way to Lima.

PERU

There's not much between the northern border and the capital. On the right was the beautiful blue Pacific Ocean, and on the left was hot, arid land with dusty cliffs. There were only a few plots of farmland, a couple of fishing villages, and one city named Trujillo. We stopped there for dinner and the night.

We arrived in Lima late in the afternoon. The Austrians dropped me off at a *pensión* near the train station, as that was how I'd be leaving town.

Lima was a gray, dingy, depressing city, and the almost ever-present thick coastal fog didn't brighten it up any. But it was the capital of the country, and that meant there were a number of museums to see. After three days, I went to the train station and bought a second-class ticket, for five dollars and change, to Huancayo.

I was traveling by myself again, but let me state that being alone is not the same as being lonely. You have to pay attention and be aware of everything. What it's really about, though, is the realization that the best place to be at that exact moment is right where you are.

I hadn't done much traveling by train, but I'd always been intrigued by it. Perhaps it was because of all the movies I'd seen of people sitting by a window as they passed through the countryside. My second-class passenger car was a well-traveled older model. The great scenery viewed through the window, however, more than made up for the rough ride.

The train line from Lima to Huancayo had to be one of the engineering feats of the twentieth century. It went from sea level to over sixteen thousand feet. A series of switchbacks cut into the mountainside helped the train reach that lofty elevation in twelve hours. In the car, an oxygen pump was provided for travelers who got dizzy from the thin air. It also got colder the higher we went.

Vassily had said that adversity provided an opportunity to learn, so I decided to give it a try. First, I allowed my negative opinion on the thin air. Thoughts of being uncomfortably cold followed, and then it dawned on me: not just fear but feelings also were initiated by judgmental thoughts. I then used a lesson Vassily said would eliminate the effects. I reviewed and studied the feelings without describing, naming, or judging them. They slowly dissolved to the point where I couldn't even remember what they were in the first place.

The train arrived in Huancayo at eight in the evening. In the morning I purchased a bus ticket to Ayacucho. Getting there was one hell of a bus trip — but "the bus trip from hell" might be a better description. We departed in an old school bus at eight in the morning. It had hard bench seats, a half-dozen broken or missing windows, and a worn-out suspension. All the passengers were Andean Indians except for me.

The dirt road we traversed was bumpy, which meant that numerous times I was bounced completely off the seat, and dusty, which meant that the air was thick with a fine Earthen powder that settled on everything, including me.

During daylight, the scenery kept me occupied. When the sun went down, it was too dark to see anything, and it got bone-chillingly cold. It was late at night, and I was bouncing up and down, covered with dust, and freezing my butt off. There was no way to get any sleep. This went on all night; in fact, the entire bus trip lasted twenty-eight hours!

However, the situation gave me an opportunity to put into practice another lesson from Vassily. He'd said, "An unfavorable situation can be transformed into a favorable one by changing the way it's viewed and judged." The precise second I changed my opinion, everything was different. I was now on an astonishing bus ride high up in the amazing Andes. The bouncing around and cold air kept me awake so I could continue to experience this once-in-a-lifetime journey. And was it ever fun!

I arrived in Ayacucho and liked it immediately. It had crisp, clean air with a bright blue sky during the day and clear, starlit nights. There was a big, beautiful plaza in the center of the 450-year-old city, where I spent several hours each day.

I was in the plaza talking to a local college student one afternoon when a bearded man walked by. My new acquaintance said he taught at the university and was a revolutionary trying to get students to join his new radical group. I took a good look at the guy. A few years later I recognized his face in a photo in a newspaper. The accompanying article said he was one of the founders of *Sendero Luminoso* (Shining Path), a guerilla group of the Peruvian Communist Party that carried on a "people's war" for years.

I asked about the best way to get to Cuzco. The answer, from the same bus company I'd arrived with, was another twenty-eight-hour trip. But they informed me the road had been closed by a landslide and wouldn't be cleared for several days. They also mentioned there were flights to Cuzco for seventeen dollars. With a smile, I knew immediately how I'd be traveling.

It didn't matter to me what form of transportation was provided. I now knew that a real traveler was always looking but didn't know for what. Being guided to an airplane that would take me to the same heights as the surrounding mountains was a great discovery.

And what a view of the Andes from the small plane! Below was the *altiplano*, the huge, flat plains that averaged between ten and twelve thousand feet above sea level. It was surrounded by rugged, snow-covered peaks that stretched to the horizon. We circled the airport before landing, and I could clearly see the town: the red-tile-roofed buildings, the narrow streets between them, and roads meandering out in all directions.

We landed, and I joyously got out of the plane. I'd finally made it to my destination: the apex of the Andes, the Incan capital of Cuzco.

A Swiss woman I'd met in Costa Rica had recommended a place to stay. The Hostál Suiza had stuck in my mind for two reasons: she'd said it was very inexpensive, and her mother was the owner. The fact that I was acquainted with her daughter must have impressed her. My small, clean room was discounted 50 percent to the equivalent of one dollar a night.

Cuzco was incomparable because I'd never been anyplace remotely like it before. Every day I'd go for a long walk in a different direction. I visited numerous Incan ruins and passed by flute-playing llama herders. I saw remarkable Incan stone walls where the rocks had been cut so precisely and fit so snugly together that it was impossible to get the blade of my Swiss army knife between them.

On a walk to the ruins of Sacsaywaman, I found that cut stones were also used to build the edifice they called the House of the Sun. Another walk took me to Quengo, a temple dedicated to Mother Earth, and to Tambomachay, a center of ancient Incan worship where the royal baths were located.

I also visited an outlying village with an Incan market. It was next to a river with the same name, Urubamba, as the group that'd recorded the music I'd heard back at the radio station in Portland. And I heard that unique, beautiful music made by Incan flutes, panpipes, drums, stringed instruments, and voices. In the village I also purchased a postcard with a picture of the busy market. I wrote "I finally made it!" on it and mailed it to the woman who let me sleep on her couch back in Napa Valley.

Early one morning I boarded a train for the three-hour ride to Machu Picchu. The "Lost City of the Incas" was considered the most spectacular archaeological find on the continent. I spent the day wandering through what was left of the plazas, temples and residences inside the walls and the terraced farms outside.

If you're ever close to Cuzco and Machu Picchu, go see them. You shouldn't miss a visit to the land of the Incas. My path, while long, was worth the effort. I'd accomplished what I'd set out to do.

I didn't celebrate, though. I knew it was just another day as a traveler, but there was another reason, too.

Several times Vassily had explained a lesson that he considered important. He'd said, "Never give yourself an ego satisfaction. Building up the ego is detrimental to understanding and experiencing higher-mind awareness. And that's what will lead you to the truth and freedom, not the ego."

After a year and a half, I wondered if my travels were over. It was an incredible adventure, so why stop? I was already in South America. The fact was I was hooked! It was the going — the travel itself — that made me want to continue. I didn't care whether there was someplace or something else to discover or not.

After three incredible weeks in Cuzco, it was time to get going again. My departure was ticketed for seven o'clock in the morning on the train heading south to Puno, on the shores of Lake Titicaca. The rail line stretched straight across the broad, flat *altiplano* and provided a spectacular view of the snowcapped mountains surrounding it.

The conductor told me the train would arrive in Puno thirty minutes after the lake came into view. Near the end of the ten-hour train trip, I got my first look at expansive Lake Titicaca. The largest body of fresh water in South America was more than a hundred miles long, and it was the highest navigable lake in the world. The shock of seeing all of that water, after traveling across the nearly barren *altiplano*, had a hypnotic effect: it was difficult to take my eyes from it.

I got off the train in Puno, found inexpensive lodging, and searched for a way to get to the Bolivian border. Several locals told me that for a few bucks, I could ride in the back of a large stake-body truck that plied the route. Next morning, I was riding beside boxes of canned food, bundles of clothing and various farm tools. Along the way, I also helped traveling Indians in and out of the truck along with their packs and bags.

Lake Titicaca was the bluest lake I'd ever seen, and it was so big no land could be seen across it. I had an open-air view as we drove the sixty bumpy miles alongside the mesmerizing lake to the Bolivian border.

BOLIVIA

This border crossing was seldom used, so there were no taxis or buses. I was still six miles from Copacabana, a small semiresort town on the Bolivian side of the lake. I'd been walking for five minutes when three Bolivian women in a station wagon gave me a ride. They said a small festival, beginning that day, was the reason for their visit to Copacabana.

I never understood what the festival was for, but at night there were colorful fireworks and dance music for the attendees. It was where I had my first glass of tasty chicha beer, made from fermented corn. I was told it was exactly the same as that made by the ancient Incas.

While sipping a glass of the brew, I recalled that the awareness process was more than just "remembering." One of the books Vassily had me read was by the Russian mystic Gurdjieff. He'd written that the problem was actually "remembering to remember" to wake up and be aware. Vassily and I had some laughs when repeating to each other, "Are you remembering to remember?"

The festival was over, and it was time to head for La Paz. At an elevation of twelve thousand feet, it's the highest capital city in the world. It's situated in a bowl-shaped canyon, with a great view from the top edge. Towering above it, off to the east, was the 21,000-foot snowcapped Mount Illimani.

La Paz was notable for seeing the unusual, such as the hats worn by the Incan women: brown English-style bowler hats. The women in Peru had all worn traditional headwear, but in Bolivia the hat of the day was the bowler. They'd been introduced by British railway workers in the 1920s. A shipment of the hats that were too small for the men arrived, so they were given away to the local Aymara and Quechua Indian women. The trend grew, and all the ladies now wear undersized bowlers cocked to the sides of their heads.

Each day I went on a long walk that always ended up in the old section of town. With the narrow, cobbled streets and small shops, it was like traveling back in time. But I wanted to see more of the country, so I took a bus south.

My initial stop was in Potosí. In the seventeenth century, the town had been known for its prosperous silver mines, but now tin was the ore excavated from the exhausted hills.

I followed that with a six-hour ride to Sucre, the old capital of Bolivia. My visit was well timed, as the market in the nearby Indian village of Tarabuco was the next day.

The best way to travel the forty miles to Tarabuco was on the strange *carril*: the wheels of an old school bus were swapped with train wheels so it could run on tracks to the village.

The market was spread over the small town. Most of the Indians were wearing colorful, traditional handwoven clothing. Some Spanish was being spoken, but the main language of the market was the indigenous Quechua. I was able to pick up a few phrases while listening to the busy villagers bartering for goods.

Sunday afternoon, while sitting in a plaza in Sucre, I was approached by an Incan Indian. He wanted to sell the poncho he held out. I studied the handwoven material with unique markings; it was clearly his work poncho. He held out his fingers, and I understood the Quechua word for five, meaning 500 bolivianos ($25 US). In my pocket was 450 bolivianos. I showed it to him and shrugged my shoulders. He hung his head and walked away. I didn't have 500 bolivianos, and it was Sunday so the banks were closed. Just as I was leaving, the man came running across the plaza. He gave me his poncho and held out his hand. I counted out 450 bolivianos and tried to convey that I'd meet him there the following day to give him 50 bolivianos more. On Monday I waited most of the day in that plaza, but I never saw him again.

I stayed in Sucre a week and then went by bus to Cochabamba. After being in South America for nearly three months, I had yet to visit any two cities, towns, or villages that were alike.

Cochabamba also had a character all its own. It's flat and spread out with a pleasant climate that was ideal for long walks. On one, I passed by numerous shops and homes flying the red banner proclaiming that freshly made chicha was available.

While taking a break and sipping a glass of the Incan brew, I reread a letter I'd received from Vassily while living in Portland. It served as a bookmark for the book I was reading at the time, so it went with me everywhere. In it he'd written, "The false self is inimical to any attempts to alter it. It fights with everything at its disposal to save its existence. Remember, you do not fight the false self, you dissolve it with constant awareness."

I'd been in Bolivia six weeks and liked it, but it was time to see what was over the next hill, or Andes mountain. At the train station I bought a ticket for the overnight train to Chile.

I was apprehensive about visiting Chile because of the military coup that'd taken place. However, negative stories about other countries I'd visited had been exaggerated by the press, so I decided to go anyway — but just for a week or two.

The train departed at eight o'clock in the morning. My compartment was in a beautiful Pullman car built fifty years earlier in Belgium. I shared it with the conductor and had it to myself all day and most of the evening.

The train first traveled south through the extended Bolivian *altiplano*. Traveling across that immense, elevated flatland and passing through the occasional Indian village kept my face at the window. After the sun had set, I paid a visit to the dining car. I shared a table with a guy from New York, the only other foreigner on the train. Barry, in his early twenties, was traveling in South America for three weeks before attending law school at Harvard. His father, a Park Avenue attorney, had financed his trip. We had a jovial conversation about whether genetics played a role in being a good lawyer.

I mentioned my plan to get off in Calama and visit Chuquicamata, the world's largest open-pit copper mine.

Barry asked if he could join me.

CHILE

After traveling through the rocky, martian-like scenery on the Chilean side of the Andes, we reached Calama and the end of the thirty-six-hour train ride. Barry and I checked into a pension and then went out for dinner and a couple bottles of delicious Chilean red wine.

In the morning we went to the office that arranged tours of the Chuquicamata mine. We were told the van used for the tour was full that day. At the radio station in Portland I'd been issued a legitimate press card with my picture on it. I pulled it out and told the man in charge that I was there on authorized business and that my companion with the camera was my official photographer. He apologized and said arrangements would be made and we'd leave in ten minutes. Barry laughed and said he was impressed with my acting.

The mine is in the middle of the Atacama Desert. There are parts of this arid region where it never rains and the wind never blows. Ancient Incan mummies found there still had skin and hair on them. In 1948, Chile and Peru fought a war for the region. Tanks were driven across the desert, and their tracks could still be clearly seen in the soft sand.

Chuquicamata was impressive and mind-boggling in size. Monster trucks carried copper-bearing rocks up and out of the open-pit mine to be crushed, separated, sent to the smelter and processed into pure copper ingots. From our vantage point up on the rim, the busy operation below looked like a toy replica.

Barry and I continued on to the capital city of Santiago. Our bus was stopped and searched half a dozen times. It was a precautionary measure because the big biennial meeting of the Organization of American States was being held in Santiago in a couple of days. All countries in North, Central, and South America would be represented by a slew of government dignitaries. Heading the U.S. delegation was none other than Henry Kissinger. I told Barry we should look for Hank, and maybe he'd invite us to lunch!

I'd been in enough countries to see that life was complicated in all of them. Vassily had once told me that people thought if something was simple, it wasn't important. "Why so simple? Can't you make it more complicated?" was how he described their logic. He concluded, "Metaphysical truths are ingeniously clear and simple!"

After arriving in Santiago, we walked over to the large OAS convention site. On a door near the main entrance was a sign that read OAS PRESS CENTER. I pointed to it, and Barry nodded his approval.

At the counter, an official asked if I was there to pick up my credentials. I said yes and handed him my press card. He checked a list provided by the U.S. embassy and told me my name wasn't on it. I said it was because I'd just arrived. He must have believed it, because he gave me a press pass and a list of activities taking place during the week-long shindig.

Being at the conference gave me a chance to continue working on something else Vassily had taught me. "It's very easy," he'd said, "to walk into a room full of people and not be noticed. The secret to being invisible is being still inside. Turn thoughts off, don't look specifically at anything or anybody, and move effortlessly."

Barry and I attended luncheons, dinners, afternoon teas, evening cocktail gatherings, and entertainment. I went on a tour of El Teniente, the world's largest underground copper mine. We also attended a meeting held by the Kissinger staff.

The week-long convention was over, and the city was returning to its normal activities. Barry had booked a departing flight, and I began wondering where to go next. That was when I discovered that my funds were low. I had enough money for a one-way flight back to California. Remembering Vassily's teaching of "don't interfere, and what you need will come to you," I relaxed and waited.

I'd found a little café that was always full of locals, and I often ate there. This day I sat next to a pretty girl whom I'd seen before. She turned to me and asked, "Do you speak English?"

"Yes, I do," I said, thinking she wanted to practice.

"Are you working here?" she asked instead.

"No, I'm not."

"Do you want a job?" she offered with a smile.

After lunch, she asked me to return to the office with her and speak to the bosses.

Their exquisite appearance told me that René, Raúl and Juan Pedro were smooth characters. They owned a company that'd secured a contract to provide English-language courses for ENDESA, the government-owned electric company. The classes would be at a brand-new hydroelectric plant up in the Andes in southern Chile. The main students were engineers and technicians, because all the manuals and blueprints for the new equipment were in English. A few classes for workers' families would also be offered in the company town.

René asked if I would like to be their first, and most important, teacher. He said lodging and food would be provided, as well as a monthly salary. I told him he was in luck: I was available and would take the job.

I stayed in Santiago for a week studying the method they used, which consisted of books, recorded tapes, and small, intense classes. After a three-hundred-mile bus trip south to Los Ángeles, I was taken up into the Andes to the new hydroelectric plant, Centrál Antuco.

Everything in my life was suddenly different, but I remembered Vassily saying, "There's nothing constant but change. Use the newness of change to wake up and be aware."

At the center of the hydroelectric plant was the company village. Some of the employees lived there with their families. Others worked a two-week shift and returned to nearby homes on their four days off. Like all the Chileans I'd met, they were very friendly.

During my stay at Centrál Antuco, the inauguration for the new facility was held. The chief engineer, Don Jorge, asked me to attend. It was a big celebration, and the guest of honor was the Chilean president, Augusto Pinochet Ugarte. After greeting the president, Don Jorge pulled me over and introduced me to him as their American English teacher in residence.

I'd been apprehensive about visiting Chile because of stories I'd read, so my plan was to only stay a few of weeks. Six months had passed since my arrival, and nearly everyone I'd met seemed pleased with their country. That was fine with me, because I liked Chile and I really liked the Chilean people.

The southern part of Chile, known as the Lakes District, was a beautiful mountainous area. I had my backpack and tent, left over from mountain climbing I'd done in Oregon, sent to me. When my five-month job was over, I headed south.

I recalled Vassily ending one of our conversations by saying, "This learning process is about the realization and experience of love. It's not the mundane definition of love that everyone thinks. It's the pure, infinite love that remains unknown to people because the ego blocks its manifestation." At that time Vassily wouldn't discuss it further. He'd concluded, "Just be aware, and don't let your mind trick you into thinking you know what it is."

My first stop was Temuco. A friend from the hydroelectric plant told me I could stay at his house there. It was a quiet town with rural activities of farming and cattle ranching.

From Temuco, I wanted to go to Argentina. A local bus took me to the road that went over the Andes, and I stuck my thumb out. The first vehicle stopped. It was four guys in an old stake-body truck with a rowboat in back. They all had big grins because they were going on a three-day camping and fishing trip. In unison they asked if I wanted to join them.

An hour later we were at a beautiful mountain lake where we set up camp on a grassy area beside the water. They were impressed that my tent unfolded out of a small bag. And I was impressed with their friendliness.

Two of them went to a nearby farm and bought a spring lamb on the hoof for food. They hung it up by its hind leg and slit its throat. One of them was below it, catching the blood in a pan. Another was cutting up onions and cilantro, which they mixed with the dark-red liquid. They all grabbed a spoon and dove in. They prodded me into trying a spoonful, and it didn't taste too bad!

On their return home, the guys dropped me off back at the road that went over the Andes to Argentina. I thanked my new friends for inviting me and waved good-bye.

I stood in the morning sun for an hour before a large truck picked me up. The driver was going to Argentina but couldn't pass through the border with passengers. He let me off a quarter mile before the Chilean border station.

While walking along, I recalled Vassily telling me it's impossible to run away from problems. He meant that literally as well as metaphorically. He'd said, "Your problems, created by thoughts, are all in your mind. And since you take your mind with you everywhere, your problems go with you as well."

I laughed, thinking, *Me and my problems are crossing the Andes and going to Argentina!* I stopped and contemplated my problems. The main one was that I couldn't control the ego-initiated thoughts that created my problems in the first place.

At the border, I handed my passport to the surprised guard who asked where I was going and how.

"Argentina, and I'll walk."

"That's funny," he said. "Wait over there in the shade, and I'll see if I can get you a ride."

The friendliness of the Chilean people also included the military border guards. Twenty minutes later a car pulled up. The guard waved me over, and I had a ride.

ARGENTINA

I jumped into the car and the driver said he was going to San Martín de los Andes, and that's where I was going. This was my first ride in a car driven by an Argentine male. Back in the 1950s there was a famous Argentinian Grand Prix race-car driver named Juan-Manuel Fangio. Almost every time a man from Argentina drives a car, he thinks he's the second coming of Fangio.

After a quick stop at the Argentinian border, the driver put his foot on the gas, and we were off like a bat out of hell. His intent showed on his wide-eyed face as he downshifted, cut a corner, and went into a four-wheel drift turn. He was in first place, and no one was going to catch him.

We arrived in the small resort town in record time. He dropped me off at an expensive hotel and drove away to pick up the winner's checkered flag. I walked away to look for more economical accommodations.

It was the off-season in San Martín, so there weren't many tourists. I stayed three days and went on hikes at Lake Lacar and in the nearby mountains. It was a peaceful area with pine forests and views of the eastern side of the Andes.

The route I chose for my return across the Andes to Chile was a little tricky. First was crossing Lake Lacar by boat to reach the Argentine border station at Paso Hua Hum. Once there, I discovered that the small, old bus to Puerto Fuy, on Lake Panguipulli in Chile, left only in the early morning. I was stuck in Hua Hum with no place to stay and it started raining. I paid a local family to let me sleep in their kitchen and caught the bus the next morning.

CHILE

In Puerto Fuy, I discovered the boat across the lake wouldn't leave until some repairs were finished.

While waiting by the lake, I realized that delays and other problems rarely bothered me anymore. Vassily had told me, "When problems such as anger, guilt, fear, or unhappiness arise, remember that those feelings are created by opinionated thoughts. Just look at those thoughts and examine them. Don't define, judge, or speculate on their outcome. Just study them, and the opinionated thoughts causing the problems will dissolve."

It was late in the afternoon when we left Puerto Fuy. The scenery from the boat while crossing Lake Panguipulli was stupendous. Rocky cliffs lifted straight out of the water and reached up to giant snow-covered mountains. The captain let me ride in the pilothouse of the boat, where the view was great. It was dark when we arrived at the small town of Panguipulli. In the morning I went by bus to the coastal city of Valdivia.

In Valdivia, I rented a room in an old Victorian house. I went on a couple of short trips to the beach at Niebla and a daily excursion to the Universidad Austral de Chile's Agricultural Department creamery. That's where I indulged in some of the best ice cream I'd ever eaten. I liked Valdivia, but the highlight of my stay was the ice cream.

Two hours south, at Osorno, was where I'd planned to take a

third route across the Andes to Bariloche in Argentina. But those plans were delayed. On the bus from Osorno to the Chilean border, I met another friendly Chilean.

Marco was in the military *carabiñeros*, stationed in Osorno. When off duty, he'd ride to the end of the bus line to be with his wife, who worked on a small farm owned by the man who also owned the bus company. The bus driver would spend the night and retrace his route the following morning back to Osorno.

Marco invited me to stay a few days at the farmhouse on Lake Rupanco. The scenery there was astonishing. We were on the north shore of the lake, and across it, pointing straight up in the sky, was the snow-topped volcano Osorno.

During my five-day stay, I went horseback riding, helped tend the livestock, picked strawberries, and had an overall great time. On the last day, I thanked my new friends and rode the bus back to the border.

I was given an exit stamp but told there was no transportation available to the Argentine border station, five miles down the dirt road. After walking for a while, I realized it was more than five miles, and not one vehicle had passed by.

Once again, I'd have to say if in 1966 someone had told me my first LSD trip in Golden Gate Park would lead to me hiking over the Andes from Chile to Argentina, I'd have said he was crazy. But when I traced events back I realized it was no hallucination!

While walking along, I pondered a profound statement Vassily had once made. "Life can only be fate, free will, or chance, or a combination of them. I'll give you some help, though. One of them can be completely disregarded. It's only when you're free from conditioned thought and fully aware that you'll be able to see the truth and realize the answer."

"Which is the odd one out?" I asked.

Vassily laughed and said, "It's chance, or as some call it, luck. It may appear to exist, but appearance is often deceptive."

I wondered about the two other life possibilities.

ARGENTINA

After walking over five miles, I reached the building manned by the Argentine army. They gave me a visa but sternly advised me not to hang around their border station. I sat down to rest anyway. The guards were about to run me off when a car pulled up. I asked the driver for a ride.

"Sure," he said, "as long as you're going to Bariloche!"

I hopped in, and it was the Grand Prix race again. We started flying down the dirt road, leaving a big cloud of dust in our wake. The driver noticed I was uncomfortable but assured me he'd driven the road many times. As if I could relax as we slid around a curve at seventy miles an hour!

The Swiss-style town of San Carlos de Bariloche, on the south shore of Lake Nahuel Huapi, is a ski resort in the winter and a cool mountain retreat in the summer. Even though it was between seasons, there were still lots of tourists.

There were good trails through the woods and around the lake. I enjoyed several long hikes, but after a three-day stay I was ready to hit the road again.

My fourth journey over the Andes was complex. First was an early morning, one-hour bus ride from Bariloche to the pier at Llao Llao. Next was a two-hour boat trip across Lake Nahuel Huapi to the Argentine border at Puerto Frías.

The officials at the border station placed the exit stamp in my passport. Nine people were going through the same procedure. A small bus was waiting to take us ten miles to the Chilean border station. From there it was another five miles to Peulla on Lake Todos los Santos.

I was first in line to ask the driver how much to Peulla.

"It's fifteen dollars, and yes, this is the only bus."

He'd anticipated my next question.

"That's too much," I said, "and you won't get it from me."

As the shocked driver and passengers watched, I slung my backpack on my shoulders and marched down the dirt road toward Chile. I had to laugh about being in no-man's-land again. What if they wouldn't let me enter either country and I was stuck in that netherworld forever?

There was beautiful scenery in the Andean pass between the two countries. Tall trees provided shade, and a gurgling stream made the music.

While walking in nature, I always listened with attention. Vassily had once taken the idea of not being able to think and see at the same time a step further: "Thinking also interferes with listening. But when full attention is paid to listening, thinking must stop. The two cannot take place simultaneously."

Listening to the sounds of water running over rocks, the breeze passing through the trees, and the different chirps from the birds kept my mind tranquil and quiet.

I'd been walking about an hour when the bus finally pulled up beside me. Everyone was applauding and cheering, and I wondered what was going on.

The driver opened the door. "Get in," he said. "I can take you as far as the border station. No charge."

I climbed in and sat down. A couple of German travelers came over, shook my hand, and said something in German.

The driver said, "A lot of people complain about the price of this trip, and I can't blame them, but nobody's ever done what you did. You walked five miles. I wouldn't have believed it unless I'd seen it.

Would you have walked the whole way?"

"Sure! But thanks for the ride anyway."

CHILE

The driver couldn't take me through the border because of the number of passengers on his manifest. The guard would count and I was the odd man out. I rode the five miles to the border, got off the bus and walked the rest of the way, another five miles, to Peulla.

I rarely got tired from walking, thanks to another lesson from Vassily. He'd told me the secret was to never carry anything in my hands, drop all mental resistance, and pay total attention to everything around me.

I discovered that the boat across Lake Todos los Santos had departed a half hour before my arrival, and the next boat wasn't until the following morning. I also learned there was no place to stay in the small village. It was another opportunity to laugh at myself and the situation.

I was standing in front of the one-room schoolhouse, scratching my head, when a young man stepped out. In our conversation, I learned Rodrigo was the local schoolteacher and another friendly Chilean. He said I could spend the night in the schoolhouse. He was also on his way to a nearby farm to purchase fresh milk and a freshly baked loaf of bread. He asked if I wanted to join him. On our way, he said this was his first teaching assignment, and I said it was an ideal location. That was how I came by my lodging, dinner, and a new friend.

Lake Todos los Santos was a beautiful lake. It had emerald-green water with heavily wooded shores. It took three hours to reach Petrohué, and it was the best of all the lake crossings I'd made in southern Chile.

In Petrohué I rode the bus by Lake Llanquihue and through the village of Ensenada to Puerto Montt and the Pacific Ocean.

I took a moment to reflect on the four different routes to cross the Andes and all the people I'd met. When you're in the middle of an adventure, you don't think about it. Thoughts interfere with the moment. While reminiscing, I realized that reflecting back didn't compare with the experience either.

Vassily had discussed something similar with me. He'd said, "When you try to understand your life and surroundings through thought, you understand it only for its importance to your conditioned mind and ego. It's your higher mind that provides the ability to see the truth. And it's self-knowledge that gives access to your higher mind."

At Puerto Montt the main thing on my mind was seafood. From its long coastline, Chile has access to numerous ocean delicacies. I indulged in two of my favorites: *machas* (clams) and broiled Chilean sea bass. For four days that was what I mainly ate.

Like a magnet, I was pulled north to Santiago. I'd missed all the amenities of the big city and was anxious to make up for lost time. I saw all the latest movies, visited museums, went to the horse races, toured several big parks, and, on my daily walks, found many out-of-the-way places to eat.

I also continued to ponder what I'd been learning. It was a challenge to wake up, be aware, and catch those uninvited, intruding thoughts as they happened. Vassily had given me an important warning. He'd said, "The ego will try to trick you into thinking you're awake and aware by merely producing a thought that tells you 'I'm awake and aware.' It'll also try to trick you into thinking you know what love is. They're both just thoughts and not the truth. Be watchful for its trickery."

Walking down the street in Santiago, I saw someone I knew: a Chilean girl who had been a student at the American school in

Costa Rica. Viviana introduced me to her mother, Mercedes, and father, Alberto. He was a diplomat with BID (Interamerican Bank of Development) in Montevideo, Uruguay. They'd just arrived for a two-week vacation at their condo in Viña del Mar. The friendly family invited me to have dinner with them.

Viña del Mar is a popular resort visited by tourists from all over South America. It has warm, sandy beaches, but the ocean, due to the Humboldt Current, is cold. Five minutes in the waves was enough for me. The beach was a different story, as it was crowded with cheerful, pretty girls in their bikinis.

I went to dine with Viviana and her parents. After dinner, Alberto asked me about my plans. I told him I'd be leaving Chile soon for Argentina and then going on to Uruguay, Paraguay, and Brazil, countries I hadn't yet visited.

He smiled and said, "Would you like some assistance with your traveling?"

He had my attention.

"I'm driving a diplomat-licensed car from BID, but I also have my own car, a Ford Mustang that's been in storage here. I want to take it back to Montevideo, but I can't drive both. Would you be interested in driving the Mustang for me? I'll pay your expenses, and you can stay at my house in Montevideo."

"When do we leave?" was my only question.

There's something about waiting for an impending journey that makes me antsy. Even though Viña del Mar was a great place to hang out, it was overshadowed by my wanderlust. For me, the actual traveling was the epitome of travel.

The delay did give me an opportunity to visit several beaches to the north and the main Chilean port of Valparaíso.

During a walk in the hills to get a view of the port, a small stone found its way into my shoe. I recalled an interesting technique Vassily had mentioned, and I decided to try it. He said, "To stay awake and aware, place a small stone in your shoe. Every time it annoys you, use that annoyance as a reminder to wake up and be aware." He then laughed and added, "It's another way of getting stoned!"

The departure time for our South American coast-to-coast trip finally arrived. Alberto drove the car with special diplomatic license plates on the front and back; I drove his Mustang with a single Chilean plate on the back. Viviana and Mercedes would take turns riding in each car.

ARGENTINA

The first day we drove over the Andes, passing by the international ski resort of Portillo. Going through a border with a diplomat was a breeze. A visa was stamped in my passport with no questions asked.

I followed Alberto through the city of Mendoza. The next big city we came to was Córdoba. Alberto wanted to have both cars serviced there, as it was less expensive than in Uruguay. A military government was in power in Argentina, and there was guerrilla activity fighting against it. In newspapers I'd seen there was usually an article about suspected guerillas being shot. Not "known" guerillas and not "captured," but always "suspected" and always "killed."

The next morning we left Córdoba. We were a couple of miles out of town when traffic slowed to a crawl. As we inched around a curve, I could see that the military had set up a checkpoint. When Alberto drove up, they saw his diplomatic plates, and he was quickly waved through. Next, the soldier in charge saw there wasn't a front plate on my car and yelled for me to stop. Six soldiers jumped in front of the car and pointed their rifles at me. Twenty more alongside the road had their guns pointed at me, too. Standing fifteen feet away, the officer in charge asked me to throw him my documents. Then it dawned on me why. If shooting started, he didn't want to get hit.

I quickly threw him my passport, and Mercedes, who was with me at the time, screamed that we were diplomats and pleaded for them not to shoot.

Just in time, Alberto pulled up. He'd noticed I wasn't behind him and had turned around. The officer ordered his soldiers to relax their trigger fingers and told us that "suspected" guerrillas were in the area.

That was the closest I'd ever been to death. As it happened, I had a strange feeling of being awake and aware and watching while the incident took place in slow motion.

I now understood what Vassily had meant when he'd said, "There are no degrees of being fully awake and aware. You either are or you aren't!"

URUGUAY

Montevideo is a large city located where the Río de la Plata flows into the South Atlantic Ocean. My favorite places to hang out were the old city, the artsy port area, and the miles of sandy beaches.

Alberto and his family were very hospitable, but a week of relaxing at their home was enough. I was ready to move on. I told him I was leaving for Buenos Aires on the slow ferry. He informed me there was also a quick flight, and he'd buy me a ticket. I said it wasn't necessary, but the gentleman insisted.

ARGENTINA

The plane, an old twin-engine DC-3, had seen better days, but it managed to land safely in Buenos Aires.

I stayed on Avenida Florida, in the commercial center of the huge city, at an inexpensive old hotel. On the famous street, a cross-section of society could be seen. High-fashion ladies, businesspeople, tourists, and the disheveled poor all frequent it. My favorite spots were the small outdoor cafés where people-watchers sipped coffee or wine.

Argentineans must be the biggest meat eaters in the world. Almost every meal has a big piece of beef as the entrée and potatoes and a salad as minor accompaniments. I'm not a big meat eater, but I admit the steaks were tasty.

Eventually the crowded city got to me, and I headed north, up the Parana River toward Paraguay. After stops in the cities of Rosario and Santa Fé, I arrived in Resistencia, a laid-back small town.

This was going to be the last place I stayed in Argentina, so a final steak dinner was in order. A small outdoor *parrilla* (grill) was recommended. I had a steak so big it covered the entire plate, and mashed potatoes and salad came with it. Add a half liter of red wine, and the dinner was complete. It was the best steak I had in Argentina, but it was the *cuenta* (bill) that was better: the whole thing cost a dollar seventy-five!

PARAGUAY

After a two-hour bus ride, a ferry took me across the Parana River to the capital, Asunción. My first impression was, *This is what a South American capital city is supposed to look like!* Asunción had a few skyscrapers, but most of the buildings were traditional Spanish colonial style.

The weather, though, was extremely hot and muggy. To deal with this, I developed a new twist on Vassily's changing my opinion of a situation. I never acknowledged or had an opinion about the heat and humidity, and they didn't bother me. I'd hear other people say, "Damn, it's hot!" They didn't realize they weren't really hot until they expressed their opinion in thought.

While in Asunción, I met some members of the Peace Corps and ended up hanging out with them. It was strange for me, as I hadn't been around anyone from the United States in a long time. In fact, I hadn't spoken much English in quite a while. Even my dreams were in Spanish.

After being with these folks, I noticed something odd. Their group mentality exhibited a narrow "I'm American" thought pattern, and they were completely unaware of it. I figured living in different cultures for so long had somehow altered my thinking and freed me from that mentality.

The revelation was similar to the insights I'd experienced while under the effects of LSD and mushrooms. Maybe it was one of those flashbacks I'd heard about but never experienced.

Then it dawned on me. I was born an American, but if I was free from that narrow thought process, what was I now? Then the realization came to me: *I'm an Earthling!* I laughed and understood, though, that due to circumstances on this planet, I had to play the game and pretend to be an American. But truthfully, I was a genuine Earthling!

I think Vassily would have been pleased, as something we'd discussed finally became clear. He'd said, "Thought creates the image of one's self, and then the individual lives as that image. So, thought is the creator of the illusion of the false self." He went on to add, "That image and illusion includes nationalism, religion, and all the social and cultural mores that go along with them."

I left Asunción and headed to where Paraguay, Argentina, and Brazil join together at Iguazú Falls. They were wider than Victoria Falls and higher than Niagara Falls, and I didn't want to miss seeing them. Since it was less expensive, I crossed the Iguazú River to Puerto Iguazú, Argentina.

ARGENTINA

I met two female travelers from Switzerland, Bibi and Ulla, when

I stopped at an outdoor café for a cold drink. They gave me directions to the inexpensive hotel where they were staying.

The next day, as I was hitchhiking the eighteen kilometers to the falls, a friendly Argentine gigolo gave me a ride. Jorge was in his midtwenties and had worked at a bank in Buenos Aires. That's where he met a wealthy, widowed, fifty-year-old client. Flora liked him, so he quit work, and they started traveling together. He'd already seen the falls but wanted to give me a tour, as he knew where to go.

And what a sight! The overall view in front of the falls was overwhelming, and the roar was deafening.

We then drove above and in back of the falls. We walked out over the flowing water on narrow wooden planks with rickety handrails. They led to a small island with a wide view of the river as it flowed toward the falls.

Jorge went to a man with a small outboard motorboat and gave him some money. He got in and told me to get in, too. I figured we'd probably go up the river a ways. But we didn't go up the river. We went down the river to the edge of the falls.

The guy turned the boat around, and I could feel the current pulling us back over the drop. I swear I could see straight down to the bottom. I opened my mouth to yell, to protest, but no noise came out. My grip on the wooden seat left dents in it.

Then everything went into slow motion. As the guy revved the small outboard motor, I noticed the machine was old, didn't have a cover, and was sputtering, sparks were flying from it, and smoke was pouring out of it like it was on fire.

Holy shit, I'm gonna die! raced through my mind.

With my eyes glued on him, the guy kept gunning the motor. Little by little, the boat fought against the current. We finally crept away from the edge and, gathering momentum, returned to where the ride began.

Jorge was shaking but tried to fake calmness. "Hey, Mike, how about that? It was fun, eh, man?"

I looked him straight in the eyes. "Yeah, Jorge, that was great. Let's do it again!"

He then saw my smile and doubled up laughing.

From that incident, death became a wise life adviser. It revealed that, invariably, one day it would win, and not knowing when taught me to live each day to the fullest. If we don't think about death, it doesn't bother us, but what it doesn't bother us to do is really live!

Jorge knew I was planning to go to Brazil and asked if I wanted to ride with him and Flora to Rio. I liked both of them, weird relationship and all, and took them up on the offer.

BRAZIL

We left in the morning and drove into Brazil. I'd now been in almost every country in Central and South America. That wasn't my original plan: this travel adventure was just how my life was supposed to be!

The terrain we drove through in southern Brazil was flat and thickly planted with sugarcane. It was the harvest season, and the fields were full of machete-wielding workers. Trucks were piled high with cut cane, and a sweet, pungent aroma filled the air.

While looking through the car window, I recalled Vassily saying, "Most people would say they're awake and aware, but they're not. The busyness of people's lives — filled with fear, frustrations, and relentless, mundane interests — keep them from seeing and experiencing the truth of their situation."

Sao Paulo, with over twenty million people, is the most populated metropolitan area in South America. Since it wasn't much of a tourist spot, we only stayed one night.

After a five-hour drive to Rio de Janeiro, we headed straight to

Copacabana Beach. Jorge said he'd always wanted to jump in the ocean there. Agreeing with him, I dove in, too.

While in the water, Jorge told me he envied all the traveling I'd done. He said he was going to take Flora back to Buenos Aires and start doing the same thing. I didn't encourage or discourage him, but I could tell it was going to happen soon. Early the next morning, they said good-bye and left town.

Vassily had given me some insight about people. He'd said, "What a person does isn't important. The essential thing is why they're doing what they do. Their truthful conscious or subconscious reason will reveal their truthful intention."

In Rio, I checked into an old hotel a couple blocks up from Flamengo Beach. It'd seen better days, but the low price included an open courtyard with palm trees.

The hotel was not far from where I rode the dangling cable car to the top of Pão de Açúcar (Sugar Loaf Mountain). From the viewing area, the beauty of the whole area could be seen — the beaches and the bay, which led out to the open sea in one direction. Turning around, I could see the busy city below. Rio may be the most beautiful city in the world, but with all the people and traffic, I wouldn't want to live there. After riding the cable car down, I went around the side to Botafogo Beach and topped off the day with a swim.

My favorite excursion in Rio was a ride on the open-sided electric streetcar. It went across the old aqueduct and up a hill to an area named Santa Tereza. Ten years earlier, I'd seen the same streetcar in the movie *Black Orpheus*. Riding it through the same neighborhood as in the movie was the highlight of my trip to Rio.

The only problem I had was with the Brazilian version of the Portuguese language. My Spanish speaking was pretty good, and when I spoke it they could understand me. But when they spoke Portuguese, I couldn't decipher a word. My laughing reply to anything they said was *"Como no!"* ("Why not!")

That made me recall a discussion Vassily and I once had. He said "Change your mind-set to loving situations that make you uncomfortable. By mentally transforming to loving them, you no longer have the problem. The negative situation will never bother you again."

I'd heard about a two-day train trip from Sao Paulo across Brazil to Santa Cruz, Bolivia, and decided to take it.

The bus ride from Rio to Sao Paulo was easy enough. The train departure would be an hour after my arrival at the station. I purchased a second-class ticket and again was surprised at how inexpensive it was for the long journey.

I love traveling by train. The countryside we passed through was rolling hills with stretches of farmland and miles of jungle — all interspersed with streams and rivers.

As we traveled away from Sao Paulo, the towns got smaller and farther apart. After dark, I went to the dining car and ordered the Brazilian specialty of *feijoada*, a black-bean and beef stew. But that only took an hour. It was impossible to sleep on the loud and rough-riding train. The only option was to wait until I was dead tired and pass out.

BOLIVIA

In Santa Cruz de la Sierra, the first thing I noticed was the cool, comfortable climate. The second was the truth to the rumor that the city was home to the prettiest girls in Bolivia.

On my initial walk around town, I saw Bibi and Ulla, the two pretty Swiss girls I'd met at the falls in Brazil. They told me they were going to Cochabamba and then to La Paz. It looked like I was also heading there, so we agreed to travel together.

We arrived in Cochabamba, and I set out to show the girls around town. We visited the central market, the plaza, and the narrow streets dating back to colonial days, and then we went to an Indian village for its weekly market. One night we went out for chicha beer and, surprisingly, they liked it as much as I did.

Something became clear to me after a couple of days in Cochabamba. I'd been there before, and I was going to La Paz, where I'd been before. If I was going to return to California by land, I'd have to go back the same way I came. Taking the same route didn't excite me.

There was another reason an overland journey might not happen: my funds were getting low. Bolivian Airlines had an inexpensive one-way fare to the United States, so that was an option.

I knew this travel adventure couldn't go on forever, and it made me remember something Vassily once described to me. He'd started with the question, "Do you know what infinity is?" I thought I did; at least I knew the word. "Look up at the sky. What you see appears to go on forever, but the question remains, is it really infinite?"

At the time, I didn't understand what he'd meant.

"The universe appears to be infinite," he said. "But is it? You'll have a great metaphysical breakthrough when you fully realize the only thing that's infinite is infinity!"

Did that mean time doesn't exist, because infinity meant there was no beginning and no end? The universe appeared to be never ending, but it was constantly changing. Maybe it only appeared that it and time were infinite. But how did that apply to me and my life?

Bibi, Ulla, and I arrived back in La Paz. The girls went their way, seeing the city, and I went mine. This was my second visit, but it was to offer two things I'd missed the first time.

When traveling, you meet a lot of people. Many are locals, a few expats, and some other travelers. Most of them you bump into at a mutual crossroads and then never see again.

My friendship with Krieger was unusual because I don't

remember when or where we met. It was like we'd always known each other. He was an aspiring journalist and photographer and was in La Paz to cover a big annual festival parade. He assured me *El Gran Poder* shouldn't be missed.

For the parade, we sat on a curb in Plaza San Francisco. It was next to cameras televising the procession throughout the country. We were also in front of the viewing stand, where the president of Bolivia, Hugo Banzer, was sitting. Just before the parade started, I stood up and turned around to take a look at *El Presidente*. He saw me looking at him, so I waved to him. He laughed and waved back.

Then the parade started, and what a procession it was! Groups of Indian women wearing colorful hoop skirts and twirling knitted balls strutted by in step, troupes of performers wearing mythical and historical costumes like the famous "devil dancers" swaggered by, and brass marching bands played march music the likes of which I'd never heard before.

After it was over, a TV broadcaster asked me what I'd thought of it. I told him it was the most astonishing parade I'd ever seen in my life.

La Paz, at such a high elevation, provided clear starlit nights. One evening while sitting on an outdoor bench, I looked up at the sky, and that mind-blowing "infinity" concept, along with "awake" and "aware," came to my attention. Then I saw it. Being awake and aware is not something that you learn is important and then never have to deal with again. To be awake and aware is a moment-to-moment necessity, one that can only be experienced right now! I wished Vassily were there so I could ask him if "now" was infinite.

I dropped by a local bar to have a beer and saw my two Swiss friends sitting with a local guy. Eduardo was a musician who played in his own jazz-rock group and was also a member of the Bolivian Symphony Orchestra. After some conversation, we discovered we had something in common.

Eduardo was interested in psychedelic, mind-expanding experiences, too. He told me about a cactus that grew locally. It was called San Pedro, and he said it was the best trip he'd ever taken. Bibi and Ulla, who were also experienced, and I voiced a desire to try it.

Early the next morning, we met with Eduardo, who had a bagful of cut-up cactus. I asked him where it grew and what it looked like. He pointed to a cactus with several arms pointing upward and said, "There it is!" I couldn't believe it. There were a half dozen of them growing near where I was staying.

We took a bus out of town to his favorite spot and our rendezvous with San Pedro. The terrain had hard-packed dirt, boulders, and sparse, dry vegetation. We walked about fifty yards and sat down on some rocks.

Eduardo told us not to eat the skin of the cactus, only the moist part below it. It wasn't long before familiar things started happening. Short gasps interspersed with my deep breaths. I was blinking to keep my vision clear. Then there was an overwhelming energy flowing through my body. That was followed by an amazing mental clarity. It allowed me to see that many problems in life were created by ignorance. All the things that people thought were necessary, like wealth and being important, were now seen as trivial and inconsequential. It was freedom from all the life impressions I'd been inundated with.

"Hey, Eduardo," I said, looking over at my Bolivian friend. "You're right. This cactus is good!"

Bibi and Ulla mumbled their approval, too. Then we all looked at each other and the laughing started. It was the pure rejoicing of being free from all the mental turmoil the world was stuck in.

Eduardo wanted to show us something, so we walked about a hundred yards to the upper edge of a cliff. It overlooked a huge canyon that was miles across and miles deep. What a view! Then I saw them: a half-dozen condors, gliding and circling in the sky. They were lifted up with the wind currents and never had to flap their wings.

As I admired the beauty of their flight, I began to hear that Incan song from the radio station back in Portland. The very one that inspired the whole journey I'd been on. Out of the blue, the name of the song came to me. It was *El Condor Pasa*, and I knew the composer had seen exactly what I was seeing.

Several hours later, as the effects of the San Pedro were wearing off, an understanding came to me. The trip was over! Not the cactus trip, but my journey to Central and South America. This part of my life was about to end, and I'd be leaving soon. I wasn't sure I wanted to return from whence I came, but the realization made it clear that was the path I had to take.

A week later I was on a Bolivian Airlines jet headed north. I wasn't sad, but I was a little tired. After all, it was the fall of 1977, and I'd been on this travel adventure for nearly three years. So I put the seat back, relaxed, and wondered what was next.

CHAPTER TEN

*"From space I saw Earth — indescribably beautiful with
the scars of national boundaries gone."*
— M. A. FARIS, *cosmonaut*

*"It is no measure of health to be well adjusted
to a profoundly sick society."* — J. KRISHNAMURTI

"MICHAEL, I can see you doing this on your own someday."
"Thanks, Captain, but there's nothin' to it. Like the
ascenders we just assisted on Andafter. All I did was watch as they
returned to true reality."

"It's still an important task, and you're getting good at it. We're
also going to see how good your prediction was that — how'd you
put it? — life on planet Earth isn't so free and easy."

"First I'll cover what happened after the goddess worshippers
were forcibly taken over by the nomadic invaders.

"Rather than return, the conquerors settled down and made
themselves at home. The climate was milder than in the far north,
and the terrain was an improvement, too. They didn't bring many
advanced skills with them, but they were quick to adapt and adopt
the new ones they came across.

"There was one aspect that didn't change though," the Captain
said in a serious tone. "They were still a male-dominated, authoritarian society, with a male, war-condoning god. Even family names
and possessions were passed from father to son, and the women and

children belonged to the male head of the family.

"So, let's look at what's happening now and see if any comparisons can be drawn. First, Earth is divided into about two hundred countries."

"The Earthlings are separated into tribes," I said.

"Yes, they are actually glorified tribes. They inhabit land that was claimed and passed down from generation to generation or land that was appropriated from another group."

"Appropriated means taken," I said. "Don't the Earthlings realize that dividing into tribes creates conflict and that conflict is the main cause of war?"

"They have yet to understand that. In fact, there are usually a half-dozen wars taking place at any given time."

"So, the Earthlings still have armies of warriors that are fighting, killing, and appropriating land. I'll have to say they're still primitive, and not much has changed."

"Some of the countries," the Captain said, "claim to fight wars in the name of peace. Their logic is that winning a war leads to peace and the end of all wars. Once in a while it does, but only for a short time."

"That's a good one," I said with a laugh. "Let me just guess that the leaders of these countries are all males!"

"You're right. They're all males. A few women have been allowed to become leaders, but they had to act and rule as a male would."

"At least if the Earthlings don't like one country, they can move to another."

"Not quite. The governments of these countries have placed restrictions on free movement."

"That's universally immoral," I said. "What do they think — they own the planet?

"They may think that," admitted the Captain.

"What happens if they reject the authority of religion?" I enquired. "Is that permitted today?"

"Most of the religions now in existence don't even allow questioning of their authority or beliefs. The guilty party usually isn't allowed to remain a member, and there is physical punishment and sometimes death for violations."

"There's more than one religion?" I interrupted. "Don't the Earthlings realize that dividing into different religious groups causes conflict and also leads to war?"

"They haven't seen the truth of that, either," said the Captain. "In fact, there are several wars based on religion taking place right now."

"Before claiming my prediction was accurate," I said, hoping I was right but also that I wasn't, for the sake of the Earthlings, "is there anything else you'd like to add?"

"There's one more issue. The Earthlings are having difficulty maintaining their environment."

"They're destroying the planet, too!"

"It's heading in that direction."

"And the reason would be?"

"It's clearly overpopulation."

"How many Earthlings are there?"

"More than seven billion and growing at a steady clip. OK, Michael, let me congratulate you. You were right. Life on planet Earth isn't so free and easy!"

"Thanks, but it's sad. It's like there's no hope for them."

"Oh, there might be. Out of this brief history you've heard, what's the main cause of their problems?"

"That's obvious, Captain. It's mental. It's their psychologically conditioned mind and ego that have them hypnotized into believing they belong to a certain tribe, country, culture, and religion. They're literally slaves to their ego and conditioning."

"True," said the Captain, "but there are ways the Earthlings can see the truth of their situation and free themselves. But that story will have to wait. New orders are coming in."

The Captain laughed and snapped his fingers, and a printout with our new orders appeared in his hands. He handed it to me.

"Where's our new assignment taking us?"

"We're to proceed to coordinates BIG1 and assist beings ready for ascending on the largest planet in existence."

"I know that one," the Captain said with a big smile. "It's the planet that was named after its founder, Hugh Munguss!"

CHAPTER ELEVEN

"What if to reach the highest place, you had to fall?"
— PETER MAYER

"I am one of those who never know the direction of my journey until I have almost arrived." — ANNA LOUISE STRONG

"Travel is fatal to prejudice, bigotry and narrow-mindedness."
— MARK TWAIN

IT WAS late 1978 when I returned to Portland, and a dark cloud engulfed me. Vassily had warned me of a forthcoming difficult time, but I'd forgotten all about it.

My friend once said, "You have to be careful not to get hypnotically drawn in by what society supposedly has to offer. The temptation of false happiness fueled by a desire for cheap or expensive thrills are all there to trap the unwary."

And that's what happened. Nothing I'd learned worked, as my ego took complete control of my life. It was strange because I wasn't even aware of being unaware. I just went along thinking I was having a good time, and everything was the way it was supposed to be.

My downward slide was fueled by alcohol and drug abuse. The drug of choice was cocaine, and I abused the hell out of it. It was easily available from people I'd previously known, and they had lots of it. That's not an excuse; it's just the way it happened. Very few days went by that I wasn't using it in every way possible. I have to admit it seemed like fun, but it took its toll on me. I lost nearly everything I owned, I lost friends, and I nearly lost my life. It took more than three years before an understanding of the situation came to me.

I'd see Vassily from time to time, but he never said a thing about my demise. One afternoon, though, our paths crossed in downtown Portland. In our conversation, Vassily mentioned his latest study of *cha do*, the Japanese tea ceremony. He told me about the Sensei (Japanese teacher), the wonderful ceremony, and what he'd learned. He never suggested I try it, but he knew what he was doing.

The following week I saw a flyer announcing an introductory course in *cha do*, and I signed up. I learned it was actually a form of active meditation. While doing the slow, deliberate ceremony, all thoughts, especially those initiated by the ego thought process, diminish and fade away. *Cha do* initiated the transformation in me, and I'll always have great respect for it.

I recalled a profound discussion Vassily and I once had. It was about why life was so screwed up and why we have so many personal problems. I asked him, "If God made us and all this, why'd he make it with so much negative and bad stuff?"

He replied, "Let's also ask what if God didn't make us and all this, and that's why it's so screwed up."

I finally came to my senses. The nightmare was over, and I sincerely thanked Vassily. He smiled and said my metaphysical learning would now return, and I was free to go wherever I wanted. Realizing what he meant, I unequivocally departed Portland. I also never used cocaine, or even marijuana, again.

It was 1982, and implementing my renewed freedom began with the initial thing he'd taught me: "Don't interfere. Be open and let what's needed come to you."

What came my way was work in the production of the Southern California US music festival. Then a move to Arizona, where I fabricated, sold, and installed microwave television antennas. There was also a job at a liquor store that specialized in imported beer. It had over four hundred foreign brews, and, as a self-imposed job requirement, I tasted all of them. I also met a recording engineer who assisted me in producing an album for a local blues band.

After a year in Arizona, I returned to Southern California and worked in a warehouse, at the shipyards, in video distribution and at the main press center at the 1984 Olympic Games.

After the Olympics, the producer of the Long Beach Blues Festival asked me to be the production coordinator of the event. It was hard work but so much fun that I did it for three years.

The practice of not interfering led me to an incident I still laugh about. I signed up for a beginning acting course at Long Beach City College but left during the first boring class. On my way out, I overheard someone say they were holding auditions for a play in the auditorium, so I paid a visit.

"I'm the director," said a distinguished-looking man. "Are you here to audition?"

Figuring there was nothing to lose, I said, "Yes, I am."

"Here are a few pages of the script. Look over the highlighted lines, and I'll get someone to read with you. Can you do an Irish accent?"

"I'll give it a try," I said.

A few minutes later a woman came over, and we read the lines. The director had been expecting someone who'd been recommended and had mistaken me for him.

"OK," he said. "You've got the part."

The play was *The Hostage,* by Brendan Behan. My character was Eustace Mulleady, an over-the-hill civil servant inadvertently in- volved in the kidnapping of a British soldier by the IRA. It was an insightful and funny play that showed the complete futility of war.

After the play, I decided to give Hollywood a try. It was a short career. I did get a few bit parts in prime-time TV shows and a couple of daytime soaps. I also did a small part with John Cusack in a movie, but it ended up on the editing-room floor. It's a tough way to make a living, and the list of out-of-work actors in LA is a long one.

In my free time, I went back over the things Vassily had taught me. It was clear that many of the metaphysical concepts I'd learned were superficial. The ego's thoughts and their implications truly went much deeper. I remembered fear was brought about by thought. It also seemed like anger, hate, sorrow, and even happiness were first thoughts in the form of an opinion or judgment.

I wanted another travel adventure and had been thinking about going around the world. Circumnavigating the planet was like a magic ritual, and did it ever excite me! The first leg of my trip around the world would be east to England.

There's nothing like the excitement of making plans for a travel adventure. Vassily shared this insight for successful planning: "The secret is secrecy. When you tell people about your plan, they're given access to your personal aspiration. With their opinion they can, and do, affect it. Even with their encouragement, the energy gets dispersed. The secrecy allows you to quietly expand and strengthen your plan."

Through the travel section of the *LA Times*, I found an inexpensive one-way ticket to London. I was ready to go.

It was 1986 when I shouted out to no one in particular, "Hey! I'm goin' around the world!"

ENGLAND

The plane landed at Gatwick Airport, and I took the train to Victoria Station. I went across the street to a pub and had my first pint of English ale.

From the start, I liked London. The tube, train, and buses made it easy to visit the museums, parks, gardens, castles and historic sites. When I needed a rest, a pub was always nearby.

It didn't take long for my love of walking to return. While wandering about the city, I met a holdover from the hippie days in London. He was a music promoter and had a half-dozen productions coming up. Most were blues bands playing in pubs, but he had one show at Hammersmith Odeon, which was a big venue. I told him about my experience, and he asked if I'd help him.

Vassily said, "It may seem like there's no end. It's a long process, but only you can discover how your psychologically conditioned thoughts control your life. You have to learn how to choose between the ego mind and your higher mind. It's not easy, but there's nothing more important."

I went on day-trips to Oxford, Cambridge, and the south-coast town of Brighton. It was winter, and my extended tour of England could wait for a warmer season.

To continue my journey, I'd been looking through the local magazines and newspapers for travel bargains. One caught my eye. A company called Magic Bus offered a one-way trip to Athens, Greece, at a very reasonable price. It was east, the direction I was going, and south, which was warmer, so I bought a ticket.

Departure was at seven in the evening on January 3, 1987, and it wasn't a minute too soon. A huge snowstorm hit London later that night. The bus down to the English Channel and the ferry was brand-new, and I thought, *This is going to be great!*

That night there were gale-force-seven winds on the famous waterway between England and Europe. If it had been gale-force-eight, the ferry wouldn't have left port. It was a big ship, but the storm was tossing it around like a toy. The passengers were being thrown about like gymnasts, and seasickness was rampant. It didn't bother me, though. I was too excited about my first crossing of the Channel.

BELGIUM

What a relief when we reached Oostende, Belgium, and terra firma. I got off the ferry and began looking for the new bus. The driver pointed to its replacement, a much older one.

Before climbing aboard, I took a closer look. It appeared to be a city bus. I instantly thought of the bus ride in Peru, but this was Europe. My skepticism increased when I stepped inside. The seats had thin cushioning and didn't recline. Since there was no alternative, I chose the seat behind the side door. At least it provided more legroom.

The other passengers were boarding, and they were all Greeks. Then the last person entered and sat down next to me. And that was how I met Manuel from Mexico City.

He was traveling around Europe for a month and riding the magic bus because it was *barato* (cheap). He couldn't believe how lucky he was to find someone who spoke Spanish.

Manuel was a funny guy and a good traveling companion. As the bus was leaving, we surveyed our situation. "At least we've got lots of leg room," Manuel said while stretching out. "But where's that cold air coming from?"

"Through that crack in the door," I pointed out.

We plugged it with a couple towels, but it was still cold. Then we discovered there was no heat in the back of the bus.

It was another opportunity to transform the situation by changing my opinion and judgment of it. I was now cruising across Europe, which was a first for me, and the uncomfortable seats and cold air were keeping me awake so I could experience the magic bus ride.

That was when Manuel and I began laughing. We knew the score and couldn't do a thing about it. The colder and more uncomfortable it got, the more we laughed. I told him about my Andes bus ride, and he told me of similar rides he'd taken in Mexico. We laughed through Belgium, and then into Germany and Austria, and then south into Yugoslavia.

YUGOSLAVIA

Manuel stopped laughing.

"Is this the Marxist country that Tito ruthlessly ruled?"

"It must be," I said.

"What'll they do to me if they find out I'm an anticommunist Mexican?"

It was our laughing that made the trip not only bearable but enjoyable.

GREECE

After three days, we arrived in Athens. The old bus had "magically" made it.

Needing an energy boost, I used the universal life energy technique. In just a short time, I was reenergized.

Manuel left to continue his European tour, and I moved into a budget hotel near the old city Plaka. I could see the Parthenon on top of the Acropolis from my room, and I wasted no time in climbing up to visit it.

It was 2,500 years old and the center of the golden age of Greece. But it was also where Socrates was condemned to death. It was a strange dichotomy, and I returned to visit it several times.

Vassily explained that the difficulties people experience are the same all over the world. No matter where they live, they go along with the flow of life in their society. He added, "The ego makes them look outside of themselves for answers to problems that are created by an internal mental process."

I liked the Plaka area. The streets were closed to cars, so it was great for walking. Small shops and restaurants were scattered throughout it, plus there was always that amazing view of the Acropolis and the Parthenon.

I met Sam, an Englishman living in Athens and an expert on the *I Ching*. He understood the sixty-four hexagrams in the Chinese Book of Changes, and we had some good conversations about them. Sam also introduced me to the best travel agent in town.

The only direction I wanted to go was east. I thought about journeying overland through Turkey, but going farther, through Iran and Russia, was forbidden. The agent told me about Bangladesh's Biman Airlines. I bought a ticket from Athens to Bombay, India; to Kathmandu, Nepal; to Dakkha, Bangladesh; and then on to Bangkok, Thailand, for an unbelievably low price.

INDIA

At two in the morning, in the summer of 1987, I stepped off the plane and into life on the Indian subcontinent. By their standards, Bombay was equated with success, at least for the haves. For the have-nots, it was living on the street.

I saw both and more: filming of one of the hundreds of movies made every year in the movie-production capital of the world; people stepping over the body of a beggar who'd died in his sleep; a snake charmer, complete with flute, basket, and hissing cobra.

I'd heard the old Portuguese colony of Goa had miles of beautiful tropical beaches. Located on the Arabian Sea five hundred miles south of Bombay, the best way to go was by ship.

The voyage took twenty-four hours and, in deck class, was inexpensive. It was comfortable, as I had room to unroll my sleeping bag on the deck. Due to the balmy weather, it was better than being in one of the small, cramped cabins.

It was during the voyage that I met Pete, a jovial Englishman. He was also on his first visit to India. We hit it off and decided to share expenses on a place to stay.

From the docked ship, we went an hour by bus to Margao and then twenty minutes on another bus to the ocean and Colva Beach. The small, quaint village had a plentiful array of coconut palm trees on a long, pristine beach.

We stayed at Jimi's Cottages, set back out of the way and run by a trio of local characters. They gave us the deluxe room with three beds. Then they offered to find us a female roommate for the extra bed.

Every evening I'd meet Pete at an outdoor watering hole and we'd watch the sunset. Our favorite beverage was soda water, fresh-squeezed lime, and *feni*, the regional firewater made from the distilled juice of the coconut palm.

At these nightly meetings I taught Pete to play cribbage. He'd never played, even though the game had been invented in England. He was eager to learn, even from a Yank! I beat him twenty-five straight times before he whipped me. His win was a call for celebration, so I ordered another bottle of *feni*.

The night before returning to Bombay, I was on the beach looking up at the starry sky when I recalled a conversation I'd had with Vassily. He said, "It may take years. It may even take lifetimes. But there is nothing more important than quieting the superficial mind and dissolving the ego. What you're learning will help you do exactly that."

I decided not to fly to Nepal. Instead, I'd go overland and see more of India. My visa was valid for three months, so there was no hurry.

The best way to travel in India is by train. Before the British were asked to leave by Gandhi, they set up an expansive railway system. The trains were often crowded, but they were inexpensive and ran precisely on time. I chose the express to New Delhi, leaving from Bombay's cavernous Churchgate Station.

I was the only foreigner in my assigned car, which was packed with passengers. It obviously provided local commuter transportation, too. Every few minutes, the train would stop and people would get off. Riding with me was a cross-section of Indian life: office workers in white shirts, women in brightly colored saris, old folks with walking sticks, wide-eyed children, beggars with tin cups, and wherever there was a crowd, pickpockets. Through the train window, I saw a myriad of city dwellers, villagers, and farmers, all going about their lives as the train rolled by.

Delhi was divided in half; Old Delhi was old, colorful and crowded, and New Delhi was contemporary and spread out. I stayed at a hotel between the two. My inexpensive lodging didn't have air conditioning, but that was OK. I preferred a good overhead fan with doors and windows wide open anyway.

On the roof of the eight-story hotel was a garden area with tables, chairs, and potted plants and trees. While checking it out, I saw an elderly Indian man doing yoga. He was doing Salute to the Sun, an exercise I did as often as possible.

Seeing the man doing yoga in the open didn't surprise me. After all, this was India, a country conducive to spiritual practice and quests.

I recalled Vassily once talking about authority. "It is important," he stated, "to question everything, including religious organizations and people who claim to have spiritual knowledge. The answer will not be found by worshipping a guru, messiah, or holy leader. The metaphysical truth of what life is about is in you, meaning that the predicament, answer, and release can be found in your thought process. Your ego will fight for all it's worth to keep you from finding the answer, but only self-knowledge will lead you to the truth and freedom."

A bus tour of old Delhi allowed me to see some unusual places. We visited the massive Red Fort, built in 1638; the Raj Ghat, where Gandhi was cremated; the Jami Masjid, the largest mosque in India; and Feroz Shah Kotla, a huge, popular cricket stadium.

The majestic Taj Mahal was only two hours by train from Delhi. The design of the Empress Mahal's mausoleum, the most famous building in India, was magnificent. It's constructed entirely of white marble. There were inlays of semiprecious stones everywhere, and the huge dome was flawless. In the main room, below the dome, a perfect echo could be heard.

"The ego constantly throws out thoughts to distract you," I recalled Vassily telling me. "They'll disrupt your attention and block higher-mind awareness. But your higher mind is always there, waiting to help and guide you. But it's you who must decide it's more important than the ego."

Going overland to Nepal allowed me to visit the ancient city of Varanasi on the famous Ganges River. The wide flowing waterway is sacred for Indians who come to wash away their sins. The numerous bathing *ghats* are steps going down to the water's edge. They're best seen in the morning when the devout are there for a sin-cleansing dip. The best view is from a boat on the river with a wide view of the *ghats*. It was incredible: women discreetly bathing in their saris next to men in their loincloths. Both were being blessed by priests for a fee or badgered by beggars seeking a good-karma donation.

The Ganges is also a popular place for Indians to come to die. They believe the river provides an instant entrance to heaven. Near the bathing *ghats* were several burning *ghats*, or funeral areas, where bodies are cremated.

The river was far from pristine. I hesitated when the boatman suggested we scoop river water up with our hands and smell it. The sweet rosewood scent was a total surprise.

Back on shore, I walked through some of the *ghats* and looked out at the river. It was several miles wide, and with the beauty of it all, I could see why it was so revered.

With my three-month visa about to expire, it was time to move on to Nepal. The trip would be in two stages. First was a ten-hour bus ride from Varanasi to the border. As we passed through the lowland, agrarian plains of India, the snowcapped Himalayas appeared on the horizon. They're the highest range of mountains on the planet, and the closer we got to them, the more impressive they looked.

NEPAL

It was after dark when we reached the border and crossed into Nepal. The final stage of the bus trip would leave the town of Sunauli in the morning. There was only one hotel, and it was the worst place I'd ever stayed in all my travels. The dozen other travelers and I complained about the dirt and smell, but to no avail. I eventually slept sitting in a chair.

The bus left early the next morning, and we drove up a hill and closer to the Himalayas. They now appeared as a massive row of jagged, snow-topped mountain peaks. Next we went down into the valley at the base of the mountain range and turned right, and a few hours later, we were in the Nepalese capital of Kathmandu.

Located between India and Tibet, Nepal — and especially Kathmandu — showed the blending of Indian Hinduism and Tibetan Buddhism. There were holy places with unusual architecture and artistic colors everywhere. I rented a bicycle and visited Durbar Square, the royal palace, a multitude of temples, the infamous Freak Street travelers' mecca, and many back roads where the daily life of the local people could be seen.

The luminous Himalayas kept attracting my attention. I thought about a trip to famous Mount Everest but decided on a trek up to Mount Annapurna base camp and Sanctuary, where the scenery was supposed to be unparalleled.

I left Kathmandu in the morning for the eight-hour bus ride to Pokhara. The small, sleepy town was the starting point for treks into that area of the Himalayas.

I'd acquired the requisite trekking permit from government authorities. I'd also use my backpack and sleeping bag on the trek. From a provisions shop, I rented a down jacket. I didn't have boots, but I decided to wear my sturdy tennis shoes, as they were better for hiking. I also brought some plastic bags to wear inside the shoes to keep my feet dry and protected from the snow.

The afternoon before starting out, I was resting and going over what Vassily had said about reflection and interfering thoughts. Then I saw it: desires were brought about by reflective thoughts. Something was seen, and then the thought of desiring it arose. Thought initiated the desire. And it was the quick and subtle process that made it difficult to observe.

The trek began with a local bus to the outskirts of Pokhara and continued with a two-hour ride in an old four-wheel-drive vehicle to the spot where the climb started. And start it did, on rocky steps, going fifteen hundred feet straight up the side of a cliff. I started out with five other people; they were obviously not in good physical condition, and I quickly left them behind. After a while my legs felt the results of climbing as well. I used the rest-step technique I'd learned from mountain climbing in Oregon, and it helped.

The second and third days were more of the same. The trail was always up, and after that, up some more. With each step, my legs were getting stronger and I shifted into a fast pace. I passed other trekkers slowly making their way or stopped altogether with sore feet, cramps, or blown-out knees.

After the fourth day, there was a reward: a large two-story house turned into a trekkers' hostel. It was owned by a Ghurka soldier who had recently retired from British service. Since it was comfortable and served good food, most people stayed put. They decided not to continue with the more strenuous two-day climb to Annapurna base camp and Sanctuary. But there was no stopping me!

At the hostel, I met three guys who wanted to make the final ascent. Two were stocky Israelis, recently released from army duty, so they were in good shape. The other, a skinny guy from Toronto, had more stamina than all of us.

We left early in the morning, and the climb was steep and difficult. There was one dangerous place where we had to cross a large ice field on a mountainside. Fast-moving water could be heard running underneath it, and we were careful not to fall through. On the second day, we reached the base camp, a three-room stone building converted into a hostel. It was also being run by a former Gurkha soldier. He was glad to see us, as not many trekkers made it up that far.

Before sunrise, we were awake and ready to leave for the last leg of the climb up to the Mount Annapurna Sanctuary. This was where the snow started to get deep, and I used the plastic bags inside my tennis shoes. The Canadian had thought of the same thing. The Israelis wore heavy boots but thought we had the better idea.

We climbed for two hours. As the sun came up, the sky turned a beautiful bright and clear blue. With my first look, I realized why this was called the Sanctuary. Completely surrounding me was one snow-packed mountain peak after another. I was over sixteen thousand feet up, but there in front of me and eleven thousand feet higher was the breathtaking Mount Annapurna peak. It was without a doubt the most phenomenal sight I'd ever seen!

I was light on my feet as I headed back down to the base camp, packed my gear, and started the descent through the valley to the lowlands. I moved quickly and wasted no time on the return. It only took me four days to reach the flat land, the four-wheel-drive truck, and the local bus back to Pokhara. The whole trek, seven days up and four down, were eleven days in the Himalayas I'd never forget.

One thing I remembered, though, was Vassily expressing the importance of never allowing myself an ego satisfaction. "The ego," he explained, "will use anything it can to enhance its false sense of importance."

I stayed a few days in Pokhara, slipping back into the casual traveler's life, before taking the bus back to Kathmandu.

I stayed in the diverse capital another week, going on bike rides, taking long walks, and playing golf at the austere Royal Nepal Golf Club.

My visa for Nepal was about to expire, so I booked my flight straight through, from Kathmandu to Bangkok, Thailand, without a layover in Dhakka, Bangladesh.

BANGLADESH

After landing in Dhakka, we were asked to exit the aircraft. I thought it was to change planes and continue on to Bangkok. But the airline informed us we'd have to wait for the next flight, which may be in a day or so. In the meantime, they'd pay for a hotel and all our meals. So I got to see some of Dhakka after all.

It wasn't a five-star hotel, but it was better than I was used to, and the local cuisine of rice, vegetables and curry was filling. The flight finally departed three days later.

THAILAND

My first impression of Bangkok, the capital of Thailand, was *What a mess!* The main streets had horrendous bumper-to-bumper traffic, but I quickly discovered it was a city full of friendly people and delicious food.

My arrival was timely. Two U.S. film companies were making movies that took place during the Vietnam era. One, with Gregory Hines and Willem Dafoe, was originally entitled *Saigon*. The other was *Good Morning, Vietnam!* with Robin Williams. They were both hiring extras. I worked two days in the former and several weeks in the latter. I was also called when Robin Williams wanted an audience to try new routines for the script. I had several conversations with him and learned we had a mutual friend, also a comedian. They'd worked together at an improvisation club in San Francisco before Robin became famous.

I also met some interesting people while filming: Bryan, who'd traveled everywhere in Asia, and "Don Juan" John, a guy who always had a pretty girl with him. I'd see both of them later in my travels.

After the moviemakers left town, there were two weeks left on my three-month visa. Since I had to leave the country to get a new one, my plan was to go down the Thai peninsula to Malaysia. I decided to take a break and visit one of the small islands on the way.

Koh Samui was a serene, tropical island that hadn't yet been discovered by tourists, and that was fine with me. I was content to be the only person on beautiful, palm-lined Lamai Beach. It was as close to paradise as I'd ever been. It rained once, but it was a treat to be in the ocean as warm rain fell and lightning flashed from huge thunderclouds just off shore.

Something unusual happened to me on Koh Samui. The island had magic mushrooms, but they no longer interested me. That revelation opened my mind for an experience that would take place later in my trip.

MALAYSIA

From Koh Samui, I went to Malaysia and got a new visa for Thailand. I only stayed two days in Georgetown on the island of

Penang, but it was so unusual that I decided to stay longer next time. It was the mesh of people — Chinese, Malays, and Indians — or actually, the different types of food available that piqued my interest.

THAILAND

I returned to Bangkok by train, and it was another great journey by rail: tropical scenery and busy villages seen from a comfortable, second-class sleeper car.

From Bangkok, I went north to Chiang Mai, a smaller and less congested city. Touring the area on a rented motor scooter, I saw an old Buddhist monastery, weavers making colorful silk material, and while riding on the back roads, the homes and friendly people of the region.

I went on a two-day trip farther north to Chiang Rai and the Golden Triangle. That's where I sat at an outdoor café in Thailand and looked across the Mekong River at Burma on the left and Laos on the right. I wanted to visit Burma, but their military government prohibited outsiders from entering.

I returned to Bangkok and enjoyed more of its sights. I rode the water taxi on the Chao Phraya River from one end of the city to the other. I went to the huge weekend market, visited the Royal Palace, and went to the horse races. For meals, I ate at one of the thousands of outdoor food stalls found throughout the city. The food was delicious and inexpensive.

I also worked as an extra in a couple of Thai movies, played a military officer in a Thai commercial, and had a role in a Danish film. After six months in Thailand, it was time to get back to traveling.

MALAYSIA

On the last day of my visa, I left for Malaysia.

The main city on Penang Island is Georgetown, which meant the British obviously had been there. Most of the inhabitants are

Chinese, but there's also a Malay community and a little India area. I bunked in Chinatown, enjoyed the tasty Malay food, especially the satay with peanut sauce, and dined in the Indian section on curry and vegetables. And I rode the funicular train to the top of Penang Hill, which had a great view of the area.

Up on the hill, looking over island life below, I recalled being with Vassily up on Twin Peaks in San Francisco looking out over city life there. It was where he'd said to me, "Fear, desire, and guilt rule people's lives. Fear makes them remain on the societal merry-go-round of life, desires keep it going around and around, and guilt distracts them so they can't get off. It's more fun to be on a Ferris wheel anyway!"

SUMATRA, INDONESIA

After two weeks in Penang, I decided to take a trip to Lake Toba, over on the large Indonesian island of Sumatra. First was a ten-hour boat trip across the Straits of Malacca to the port city of Medan. That was followed by a three-hour bus ride in the mountains to the lake. Toba is the biggest lake in Southeast Asia and the largest crater lake in the world. It took an hour by boat to reach the crater island of Samosir and the village of Tuk Tuk.

From the guesthouse where I stayed, there was a great view of the dark blue lake. On walks I saw decorated A-frame houses that the locals lived in and visited a hot springs for a soak.

The day before departing, I ran into "Don Juan" John from Bangkok. He was also leaving, and we decided to travel together to Singapore.

SINGAPORE

The city-state of Singapore was the cleanest place I'd ever been, the result of stringent cleanliness laws that are strictly enforced. Even chewing gum is illegal. The mastermind behind the Asian economic powerhouse gave a speech on TV. The quasidictator Lee Kuan Yew assured his citizens that happiness wasn't free speech and democracy, but rather lots of money for extravagant purchases. It must have worked, as he was very popular. My pack of Chiclets remained well hidden.

My favorite place in Singapore was the famous Raffles Hotel. It's named after the British founder of the country, and it's where I drank a mandatory Singapore Sling.

JAVA, INDONESIA

John and I decided to continue on to the exotic Indonesian island of Bali. Direct flights were expensive, so we took a cheaper flight to the capital city of Jakarta on the island of Java. We'd then go by train and bus to Bali. Our rationale was that we'd save money and see more of the island.

We stopped in Yogyakarta, the artistic center for the island of Java. During a week's stay, I saw a dazzling Ramayana dance presentation, wandered through the colorful bird market, and bought a shirt made from the region's batik material from an artisan. It was a good visit, but I was anxious to get to Bali.

BALI, INDONESIA

The majority of the people on Bali are Hindus, but the island belongs to Indonesia, the most populated Muslim country in the world. It's unique for other things, too.

After arriving in the capital city of Denpasar, I immediately went to the budget resort area of Kuta Beach. The expensive five-star resort area of Sanur was five miles away on the other side of the island's southern peninsula. Kuta had a nicer beach and more to do, and it was a fraction of the cost. My hotel didn't have air conditioning or a swimming pool, but there was a beautiful beach and the ocean. And my room with a palm-shaded porch, where breakfast was served to me, cost only five dollars.

Kuta had two drawbacks: at the beach was a mob of hawkers constantly pestering everyone to buy this or that, and Australians had overrun the place and wanted to turn it into Aussie-land, complete with Kangaroo Bar and Koala Café.

There was a trick Vassily told me to use when confronted by bothersome people. "If someone is pestering you, just raise your awareness, and they'll disappear. They need a terminal that supplies a reflection back to their level. When they don't get it, they lose interest."

Wanting to see more of the island, I rented a motorcycle at four bucks a day for two weeks.

My first destination was the village of Ubud, up in the hills. There was a main thoroughfare, but I chose the quieter back roads and quickly learned that renting the motorcycle had been a great idea. With no traffic, I casually rode past rice paddies and palm trees and through the occasional small village.

I remembered 1966 and that special day in Golden Gate Park. If someone had told me my first LSD trip would lead to a motorcycle tour of Bali, while I was on a trip around the world, I'd have said they were crazy. But insane as it would've sounded, that's where it led.

Ubud is the cultural and artistic center of Bali. There are numerous galleries and shops selling woodcarvings, leather crafts and paintings by local artists. One evening I saw a performance of a traditional Balinese Legong dance with Gamelan music. The multicolored costumes, with gold embroidery and jewelry, accented the exotic performance.

Near where I stayed was Ubud's infamous monkey forest. A thick growth of trees was home to a mischievous band of monkeys. They were always ready for an edible handout, but if you weren't careful, they'd snatch anything else you had. I laughed, as the monkeys were a good reminder of the importance of being awake and aware.

Vassily had once said, "People don't realize that the answer to their problems can be found only when they're awake and aware. The ego uses desire, initiated by thoughts, as a distraction to what is happening in their life. They think their problems will be alleviated by acquiring something or having someone that'll make them happy. It's necessary to study desire, to understand it, and be free of it."

While cruising up to the volcanic lake of Batur, I came across the ruins of Pura Kehen, the eleventh-century Temple of Fire. It was deserted, but steps rise steeply to the remaining three levels of stone structures and gardens. For its age, it was in surprisingly good condition.

After passing through two small villages, I finally reached the summit of Mount Batur. There was a good view of the small lake in the volcanic crater. It was worth a look, but I decided to continue on to the north end of the island.

It was a winding, downhill road all the way to the Java Sea. I rode through the port town of Singaraja and then went another ten miles to the small beach resort of Lovina. Because it's off the beaten track, few tourists visited it. The black-sand beach with coconut palms and beautiful sunsets was quiet and peaceful.

I lazed away a few days at Lovina, then decided to ride around the north side of the island on the road that hugged the coast. With the ocean on my left and hills on my right, I passed through six villages. Apparently not many outsiders had been there. When I'd stop and look around, villagers would inform those indoors, and soon everyone was outside looking at me.

I cruised through the town of Amlapura and then headed to the southeast of the island and the secluded beach village of Candidasa.

It was quaint and quiet but wouldn't be for long, as hints of expansion were visible everywhere. The small white-sand beach was accessible only at low tide. At high tide, I headed for the hills behind the village where there was a great view up and down the coast.

My calendar said it was time to return the motorcycle. Back in Kuta, it was as lively as ever. There were scads of tourists, a few travelers, and lots of locals to make a buck off both.

There was a week left on my visa, and Indonesia didn't grant extensions. With so many Aussies in Bali, I thought airfare might be cheap to their country. After checking, I bought a bargain ticket to Perth. I'd met a girl in Goa, India, who was from Perth. She'd raved about how it was the best place in Australia. She'd given me her address and phone number, so I sent a postcard telling her I'd call to say hello. On the final day of my visa, I boarded a Quantas jet and was off to the "Land Down Under."

AUSTRALIA

Perth immediately reminded me of some place I'd been before but couldn't identify. After checking into a hostel, I called the girl I'd met in India, but she wasn't there. She was in London. Her brother Derek had received my postcard, and we had a nice chat. He said he had a spare room and asked if I wanted to stay with him.

I'd met a lot of friendly people on my travels, but I never talked about metaphysics with anyone who didn't mention it first. Vassily was correct when he'd said, "There's a big difference between learning and realizing. Learning is memorizing and takes time. Realizing is an immediate experience. Realization comes from your higher mind as an instant insight with true understanding."

Derek's house was located four miles from the city center in a suburb. The center area was closed to vehicular traffic and had lots of shops, places to eat, and buskers (street performers) entertaining the pedestrians.

Close by was Kings Park, with miles of hiking trails. From a hill there was a great view of the wide Swan River. It flowed on for twelve miles to the port city of Freemantle. On a visit, I found it was older than Perth, had a museum about the original English inhabitants, offered delicious seafood, and provided a good view of the South Indian Ocean.

While looking over the water, it came to mind that Vassily had been correct about the difficulty in maintaining awareness. He gave me techniques to try but said I'd have to come up with personal ones that worked for me. There were a few that worked for a while, but none lasted. "You'll find that a technique will work for a while," he suggested, "and then its ability to keep you aware will diminish. The ego, or false self, is very cunning and adaptable. It will slowly distract you from your goal of maintaining an aware state of mind. Learning the ego's tricks leads to a deeper understanding of how your mind works."

One afternoon Derek took me for a beer at a microbrewery in Freemantle. He drove the scenic route down to the ocean and along the coast. The beaches in Perth looked familiar, and it finally dawned on me what this place reminded me of: Southern California! The beaches, the climate, even the houses and streets had a SoCal appearance.

I stayed in Perth a month and then decided to return to Asia. It was easy to book a flight deal. The route went from Perth to Bangkok, to Hong Kong, and finally to Los Angeles. It was inexpensive and the ticket was valid for a year.

Even though I'd been on my around-the-world adventure for nearly two years, it felt like there was something else to do. That's why going back to Asia felt like the right move. After thanking Derek for his great hospitality, off I went.

THAILAND

Returning to Bangkok was like a homecoming, and I settled back into the same routine. I contacted the people from the film and TV business, and got jobs in a Thai movie and a commercial. There was a problem, though: I'd done it all before.

I met a fellow traveler who'd just returned from southern Thailand. He told me about a Buddhist monastery that held monthly ten-day meditation retreats. The monastery was well known in Thailand. It was on a forested hill and was something different, so I decided to visit Wat Suan Mokkh (garden of liberation).

After walking into the hillside wat (monastery), I immediately noticed how cool and peaceful it was. I saw lots of shade trees and twenty-five unobtrusive buildings.

The head monk, Buddhadasa, was the founder of Suan Mokkh. He was known for writing scores of books based on his scholarly knowledge of Buddhism and Pali, its original language. Combining it with Buddhist meditation gave him a profound understanding of the teachings of Buddha. Many worldly scholars agreed he knew more about Buddhism than anyone on the planet.

During an introspective five-month stay at Wat Suan Mokkh, I realized that Buddha was the most intelligent person I'd ever come across. He was the first psychologist and had come to a comprehensive understanding of how the mind functioned. He realized how the suffering experienced by humans was caused by the repeating cycle of events in its mental processes. He also saw a weak link in the sequence that provided an escape from continuous mental enslavement. The rest of his life he taught how *nibbana* (also called *nirvana*) — freedom from suffering and liberation — could be attained. I understood a lot of it, as it coincided with what I'd learned from Vassily.

At Wat Suan Mokkh, Buddhadasa continued the tradition. He gave instruction in *anapanasati* (mindfulness with breathing contemplation) and *vipassana* (insight meditation).

I attended four retreats where they were taught. There was sitting and walking meditation, and nightly one of the three Western monks in residence gave a *dhamma* talk. *Dhamma* is the secrets and truths of nature.

One of Buddha's beliefs caught my attention: the impermanence of everything. From it I realized that all desires are for impermanent things. At the wat, monks were sent to a morgue to meditate on a corpse and the impermanence of the body. But I had a question: infinity appeared to be the only thing that wasn't impermanent! The monks gave me a serene, knowing smile when I asked them about it. They encouraged me to continue my meditation on it.

Thanks to my stay at Wat Suan Mokkh, I had a better understanding of what Vassily had taught me. Higher-mind awareness, which the Buddha called *nibbana*, was true freedom from suffering. Vassily had said, "Being awake and aware will allow your higher mind to show you the truth and thus eliminate difficulties and problems in your life."

My stay at the wat was over, and I thanked the monks for everything. Before leaving, there was one thing I wanted to do.

I'd often visited the oldest meditation building at the wat. On its walls were Buddhist pictures, painted and drawn by resident monks, and writings in both Thai and English. Many times I'd sat in front of a saying written forty years earlier by an American monk. Before leaving, I wanted to copy it down. I wrote, "Oh Boundless Joy, to find at last there is no such thing as happiness in this world." I quietly contemplated the idea that happiness is impermanent: it comes and invariably goes, leaving misunderstanding in its place. To completely let go of all deceptive desires for happiness brought freedom and true joy!

I'm not a Buddhist. I don't bow to statues, light incense, chant, or make weekly visits to a monastery. But, as I understand it, that would be OK with Buddha, as the most important thing to him was to learn the truth and reach liberation. And that's what it's all about.

There was a month left on my visa, and I had enough money left for a final vacation on the islands in the Gulf of Thailand. It was a fifty-mile bus ride to the city of Surat Thani and then a two-hour trip on the passenger ferry to Koh Samui. Having already been there, I decided to go to the next island over, Koh Phangan. The only visitors to it were hearty, knowledgeable travelers.

To get there, I rode in a passenger-carrying pickup truck from the main ferry port of Na Thon over to Ban Bo Phut on the north side of Koh Samui. Then a boat took me on the hour-and-a-half voyage to the short pier at Thong Sala on Koh Phangan. From there, a small motorboat transported me along the south coast of the island, around a jutting cape, and north to the beautiful, little bay and beach at Hat Rin.

The long, sandy beach, lined with coconut palms, was an ideal place to lie in the sun and relax. I rented a small bungalow steps from the water's edge. The only electricity was produced in the evening by generators at two open-air restaurants. I stayed three wonderful weeks at the island paradise. Finally, time came for the journey back to Bangkok and preparation for my return to California.

I made a reservation for a flight all the way through to Los Angeles. I could have stopped over in Hong Kong, but I decided against it, as my funds were nearly gone. I made a note to put it on the itinerary for my next travel adventure.

The time real travelers dread more than anything, and never talk about, had arrived: I was out of money and had to return from whence I came!

I boarded a plane for the seventeen-hour flight across the Pacific. It was 1989 when the plane landed in Los Angeles. With a big smile

I said to the immigration officer as he stamped my passport, "Hey, I went around the world! It took me three years, but I made it."

I immediately started thinking about where my next trip would take me and what I'd learn while on it, as there was no doubt I'd go again.

CHAPTER TWELVE

*"If there is any religion that could cope with modern
scientific needs it would be Buddhism."*
— ALBERT EINSTEIN

*"It is better to conquer yourself than to win
a thousand battles."* — BUDDHA

"SO, WHY did they name that huge planet after that guy?"
I enquired.

"Because he was its founder and his name was Hugh Munguss,"
said the smiling Captain.

"It certainly dwarfs Earth. And speaking of that planet, you said
you'd reveal how you became interested in it."

"It started," the Captain said, "with new orders. I was sent to
sector NO1 to assist a being from Earth who was nearly ready to
ascend. I arrived and saw the man sitting in the shade of a large tree
with his eyes closed."

"So what happened?" I impatiently asked.

"Not wanting to startle him, I cleared my throat to get his
attention. He opened his eyes and smiled. I told him I was a guide
and there to assist him in returning to true reality.

"Because it was my first visit to Earth, I recorded it. If you'll
watch the screen, Michael, you can see what happened."

The Captain and the man appeared on the screen.

"Are you ready to go?" asked the Captain.
"You'll have to wait awhile," the man said.

"What?" I blurted out. "Why'd he say that?"

"How long do I have to wait?" asked the Captain.
"Until I've completely overcome the final temptation of maya, or illusion."
"Is it a difficult thing to do?"
"You're not familiar with the situation here on Earth, are you?"
"Well, truthfully, not the details."
"Do you have the ability to learn about it?"
"Yes," said the Captain. "Is it important that I know?"
"If you want to understand what's going on here."
"OK, but before I research it, what's your name?"
"It's Siddhartha Gautama, but it might change."

I turned to the Captain and asked, "What did you do?"

"I went to the archives to find out what the situation was on the planet."

"Is that how you learned what's happening there?"

"That was my introduction. After analyzing the history of life on Earth, I had an inkling of why there weren't many ascenders from the planet."

We looked at the screen again, and the Captain had returned to where the man was still sitting in the shade.

"Do you now understand the situation here on Earth?" asked Siddhartha.

"Somewhat," the Captain replied. "The problem for Earthlings is mental and has to do with their ego and subconscious memory. Their psychological condi-tioning appears to be so thorough that they aren't aware they're in a mentally controlled state. It looks like you found a way to free yourself, though. How'd

you do it?"

"Let me start at the beginning," said Siddhartha. "I was born a prince in a small, wealthy kingdom. I led a protected life, and it wasn't until I was twenty-nine that I discovered that all humans suffered from mental, emotional, and physical pain and death. To learn the cause of the suffering, I left my family and kingdom. First, I studied with spiritual masters. While I learned a lot from them, they didn't give me the ultimate answer.

"Next, I tried self-discipline, including fasting, but that didn't provide the answer either. So I decided to sit in the shade of this big tree until I figured the whole thing out. As I meditated, a realization came to me. It began with understanding how the mind functions and how it creates the illusion of the false self. I started with suffering and went backward to find where it originated. After realizing there was a repeating sequence of events, I saw it had a weak link. Because of birth, there was obviously a body and mind. Because of body and mind, there were the five senses and thought. The five senses and thought create the false self. The false self creates further thoughts of judgments and opinions that lead to feelings and contact. The feelings and contact cause desires. When the thoughts that initiate those desires occur, don't attach or cling to them. Just be mindful and watch them. They'll disappear and the desire won't take place. That starts the demise of desire, suffering, and the false self. The important effort is to be mindful."

"You've done it," said the Captain. "So why do you want to stay?"

"So I can show others how to develop mindfulness. They'll be able to see the impermanence of all the things they think will make them happy. They'll be able to discover the truth and find their way to the ultimate freedom of nibbana. And that's why I want to stay, at least for a while."

"What a dilemma for you," I said, sitting on the edge of my seat. "Now I understand what you meant by important decisions. What did you do?"

"I wrote on the orders, 'DELAYED DUE TO EXTENUATING

CIRCUMSTANCES.' Then I filed them away until he was ready to return to true reality."

"Did he accomplish his goal?"

"He compiled an accurate description of the humans' mental problem and detailed how to escape the enslaving predicament."

"He said his name might change. What did it change to?"

"His followers named him the Buddha," said the Captain. "It means 'to awaken,' but in his case the word means 'Enlightened One.'"

"Were there other teachers like him?"

"There was another Earthling who amazingly added to the Buddha's realization. He was also a great teacher. His role, however, became distorted and his teachings were altered. But that story will have to wait."

The Captain laughed and snapped his fingers, and a printout with our new orders appeared. He handed it to me.

"Where're we going this time?"

"We're off to sector H20 and one of the Drayt planets," I said.

"Which one is it?"

"The one that's elevated and completely covered with water."

"Oh, sure," said the Captain with a smile. "That has to be High Drayt!"

CHAPTER THIRTEEN

"A good traveler has no fixed plans and is not intent upon arriving." — TAO TE CHING

"The unaware life is not worth living." — SOCRATES

IT WAS 1990, and my around-the-world travel adventure had been successfully completed. It was time to squeeze back into the societal menagerie.

I found two jobs. On weekdays, I worked at an Air Force base renovating buildings. On weekends, I sold high-quality, fashionable furniture.

The two years I worked gave me an opportunity to practice the active meditation I'd learned from cha-do. When being aware and paying total attention to what I was doing, ego-initiated thoughts couldn't interfere.

I'd learned a lot from LSD, Vassily, Buddhism, and traveling. It seemed like my new task was fitting them all together, like a jigsaw puzzle.

When the time came for another travel adventure, I hadn't decided where to go. I'd always liked working in other countries, as it didn't seem like work.

From a newspaper article, I learned there were a lot of foreigners teaching English in Japan. The cost of living was expensive, but teachers' wages were high as well. It sounded good to me, and I'd never been to Japan.

I found an inexpensive flight on Taiwan's China Airlines. It went from LAX to Tokyo and then to Taipei, Taiwan. For an extra fifty dollars, I added stops in Hong Kong and Bangkok.

My timing was perfect, as the owner of the furniture store where I was working held a going-out-of-business sale and retired.

At the Air Force base, I had six weeks of vacation coming. They couldn't believe it when I told them I was going to Japan and wouldn't be returning. I just laughed and said, "Sayonara!"

My boss, a sergeant, was transferring to northern Italy and laughingly told me to stop by if I was ever in the area.

JAPAN

The flight landed at Haneda Airport in the middle of Tokyo. From the air, the big city looked confusing. Several straight highways could be seen, but the other roads went angling off in every direction.

My first few days in Tokyo, I walked around a lot to get oriented. Then I rode some of the subways and trains. It reminded me of my old saying, "I may not know where I am, but I'm never lost!"

I looked for a teaching job, but I'd arrived after the school year had started so all the good positions were taken.

It brought to mind a conversation I'd had with Vassily. "Life will be easier when you truly understand your problems. That means knowing how your lower mind works and how that process causes your negative situations. That's when you use your higher mind to respond and eliminate those problems."

I responded by going to a club that was a hangout for *gaijins* (foreigners). And that's where I met an interesting character. Max had been in the marines and done undercover work infiltrating subversive groups. He'd been promised a reward and promotion, but they reneged. He was in Japan when he checked out of the military. Not wanting to return to the United States, he stayed and learned the language.

I gave him a rundown on the places I'd been and the things I'd done and ended with my problem of finding a teaching job.

"You don't want to teach English," Max advised. "It's boring. I work for an agency that does casting for TV, films, and commercials. They're always looking for a Westerner to play a businessman, and you've got the right look. I'll tell you what to do; just buy us another beer."

"Two cold Asahis comin' up!" I replied.

I visited NTT (Nippon Telegraph and Telephone) and bought a small pager called a "pocket bell." And I signed up with Max's agency, and they gave me a job the next day.

I played a businessman on a TV program, and Max was there to interpret. It was fun, and the pay was much more than I expected.

I also signed up with nine other agencies. After learning I'd been an actor in Hollywood, they all promised to call me when something was available. I received calls for work almost daily, and Max was right: it was a lot more fun than teaching English. Twice I was cast as a businessman arriving in Tokyo by helicopter. Both times, the director, producer, and I went up for a view of the huge city.

Several acting jobs came with speaking roles. The directors had me speak in English and then added subtitles in Japanese. I also had a role in Japan's popular soap *Kimi No Nawa*. And I was cast as the Swedish coach for a famous Ethiopian long-distance runner in a documentary for NHK (educational TV).

On days off, I took short trips outside Tokyo or explored the city. I went to Yokohama, Mount Fuji, and Hakone, famous for its hot springs. In town, I went to the peaceful gardens at the Imperial Palace. I also visited the upscale Ginza shopping area and the discount electronics paradise of Akihabara.

Vassily had conveyed something I didn't comprehend at the

time. He'd said, "What you see and experience in life is similar to looking in a mirror. It's a reflection, or actually, a projection from your subconscious mind. When you realize this, a much higher level of learning will begin."

The best job I had in Japan was at Christmas. Max asked me to work on a job he did every year: playing Santa Claus at the Tokyo horse racetrack. The first day, there were looks of surprise as bettors were met with a "Ho-ho-ho, Merry Christmas" from a rollicking Santa. The second day, it was easy to tell who'd won money the day before. They smiled and returned the greeting, but the losers avoided me like the plague!

After work, Max suggested we walk through the narrow streets and have a few beers to celebrate the good payday. On almost every corner in Tokyo, there's a vending machine dispensing small to extra-large cans of cold beer. Max said he'd walked from one end of Tokyo to the other more times than he could remember. That evening we visited more vending machines than I could remember!

What Vassily had said about the subconscious and projections from it still wasn't clear. He said it was one of the most important realizations in metaphysics. I kept open, though, hoping to learn more about it.

The six months I lived in Tokyo were fun, but it was time to move on. The prospect of going to another place I'd never been before was all the incentive I needed to pack my bags and head to the airport.

TAIWAN

I stayed at a small hostel used by local English schools as a source for teachers. The first day, the school next door asked me to teach an advanced conversation class, a beginning class at a business office, and a public-speaking class at Citibank's main office. I didn't need the money, but it was a good way to meet people.

I like living in a different culture. It wanes, though, when everything becomes familiar. That's when being in a place too long sets in, and two months in Taiwan was long enough. Besides, last time I'd promised myself to stop in Hong Kong, and it was next on my itinerary.

HONG KONG

Landing at the old Kai Tak airport in Hong Kong was the highlight of the flight. The plane made a steeply banked ninety-degree turn just before touching down. It was flying so low that I could look in the windows of the apartment building beside the airport and see what TV programs the occupants were watching.

I stayed in the popular Tsim Sha Tsui area on the tip of Kowloon Peninsula. I thought Tokyo was crowded, but there are more people per square mile here than anywhere else in the world. Most were of Chinese ancestry, but there were also contingents from India, the Middle East, Africa, Europe, the United States, and, of course, England.

Hong Kong is a shopper's paradise, with thousands of stores catering to tourists. There were several large, low-priced night markets selling everything imaginable. I took the Star Ferry across Victoria Harbor to Hong Kong Island and rode the tram up to Victoria Peak for the great view of the island.

While in Hong Kong, there was a change of plans. Since I'd never been to China, the decision to change direction and apply for a three-month visa was easy. I decided to go to Shanghai by ship. It was a three-day voyage, and of the seven travel classes, sixth was the best buy.

The only place to purchase tickets was at the Chinese Government Travel Bureau office. While buying mine, I discovered they also sold tickets for the trans-Siberian and trans-Mongolian trains. I was dreaming about traveling from Beijing to Moscow for seven days when it dawned on me: nothing was keeping me from it. So I bought an inexpensive one-way second-class sleeper ticket. The reservation was for the last day of my three-month visa for China. Wow! I was not only going to Shanghai and Beijing, but Moscow, too.

Vassily had told me the untrained mind is always analyzing everything. It initiates opinions and judgments based on its psychological conditioning. He'd said, "People's minds are occupied with thoughts about everything all the time. That's what distracts them from learning how their minds work. Realizing life is a mental projection is what self-knowledge is all about."

Before leaving, I was in the infamous Chungking Mansion highrise and saw my friend Bryan from Bangkok. He was working there and said to write him in care of the Tsim Sha Tsui post office, as there might be a job for me, too. He didn't give any details, but I promised to keep in touch.

SOUTH and EAST CHINA SEA

The ship to Shanghai was great. The sixth-class cabin had eight comfortable bunks. I shared it with two Brits and a Dane, so there was plenty of room. The ship had a large entertainment room, a bar, a big dining area, a library and long, wide decks.

Of all the passengers aboard, one stood out. He was tall, in his midtwenties and attired like a Haight-Ashbury hippie. In a chat with the fun-loving, free-spirited Basel, I learned that he'd graduated from a university in Utah, he'd lived in Taiwan for several years, and he was fluent in Mandarin, the dominant language in the majority of China. Although we didn't discuss traveling together, we ended up doing just that.

CHINA

I'd read about the wild past of Shanghai, but it was now in the process of commercial expansion. New buildings, stores, and hotels were going up everywhere. There were still some parts of the old Shanghai that could be visited, though.

One was the old French Concession area, which was a misnomer as no French folks ever lived there. Basel and I walked through the old Chinese city, a fascinating maze of narrow lanes lined with cramped, closely built homes and shops. It was where the Yuyuan Garden Park and the bazaar market were located.

On the "miracle mile" shopping street of Nanjing Road, there were numerous places to eat. My favorite was a bakery next to the historic Peace Hotel. Just down the road, we attended a rousing performance of the amazing Shanghai Circus.

We decided to go to the more tranquil city of Suzhou, an hour and a half away by train. It's a major silk-production center also known for its canals and gardens. We rented bicycles and rode to the North Temple and its tall pagoda, which was nine stories high and made of wood. We climbed to the top and had a panoramic view of the entire city.

A funny incident happened while we were walking through the crowded nightly street market. Basel was friendly, and the Chinese loved the colorfully dressed guy. We stopped at the table of a vendor whose specialty was underwear. There were men's, women's and children's in many different styles, colors and sizes. The two salesgirls smiled as they watched Basel search through the undies. He picked up a pair and said in Mandarin, "How much are the hats?" The girls doubled over in laughter. Basel asked if he could see their largest hat, and if it was OK for men to wear women's hats. He continued asking about "the hats" as a group gathered around him. We had to extricate ourselves from the crowd, but as we looked back, they were all roaring with laughter.

We decided our next stop would be a Chinese-style adventure: a visit to the town of Tai'an to climb the sacred Taoist mountain of

Taishan. Getting there was an adventure, too.

Basel, using his university ID card, purchased discounted student train tickets for us. The upside was that we paid the same amount the locals did, which was a fraction of the tourist price. The downside was we had to travel in the third-class car. Picture this: It was an overnight ride on uncomfortable, hard seats with loud Chinese music playing all night. The bright lights never went off, and the car was full of Chinese indulging in their unhealthy habit of chain smoking, continually hacking and coughing, and incessantly spitting on the floor.

The situation, however, did bring to mind a Vassilyism: "When people judge, blame, or have a negative opinion about something or someone, they're frequently guilty of the same thing they're criticizing."

"How does that happen?" I asked him.

"Invariably, they mentally project the conditions from their past from their own subconscious on to others. Their criticism is correct, but they're really criticizing themselves in a previous situation."

His words prompted me to change my opinion and transform the setting on the Chinese train. It worked, as I actually started enjoying the bizarre scene.

The town of Tai'an was where the ascent to the summit of Taishan began. We'd do it at night in order to be on top to catch the first glimpse of the sun at daybreak. Sunrise was at five in the morning, and the hike would take six hours, so we decided to leave at about ten the night before.

The Chinese climb Taishan because of myth, history, and religion. They believe that those who make it to the top will live to be a hundred. Emperors have climbed it and so did Confucius, and now it was our turn.

It was dark when we reached the summit. We went to a high spot and waited. The sky in the east began to brighten, and then, from behind the distant, dark mountains, the first blip of the sun appeared. It was a brilliant sight, and I immediately understood why Taishan was sacred and why people climbed it.

We took the overnight train to Beijing, this time in a second-class sleeper, and arrived at Xizhimen (north) train station. For our initiation to the Chinese capital, we went to a famous restaurant for Peking duck, and it was delicious.

We both wanted to visit the famous Great Wall. Over two thousand miles long, it stretched from the east coast all the way to the Gobi Desert. I climbed to the top and found an elevated roadway. It snaked up, down, and around the rolling hills for miles.

Basel decided to return to Taiwan to look for work, so I was on my own again. I used two types of transportation to get around Beijing. The subway was inexpensive, and each stop provided a new area to explore. The other was what the Chinese used: a bicycle. Broad cycling lanes lined every major street. My rented two-wheeler took me down the wide boulevards, up the back streets, and into hidden alleys. This was how I saw Beijing from the inside out.

I rode by the famous Tiananmen Square, where Mao Tse-tung's mausoleum is located. I went through it but thought his face looked like a wax-museum figure.

Surrounding Tiananmen were many important buildings with unusual names: the Great Hall of the People, the Monument to the People's Heroes, the Chinese Revolution History Museum, and the Heavenly Peace Gate. The latter was in front of the Forbidden City: a good name for a place that was off-limits to the Chinese people for five hundred years.

My bike rides took me to several large shopping areas. I visited one to practice saying numbers in Mandarin. Haggling on prices with the merchants was the norm. My problem was choosing a nice leather jacket to bargain on. Even though it was the middle of summer and a hundred degrees, I had to buy it. The negotiated rock-bottom price was only twenty-three dollars!

My preparation for the seven-day train trip to Moscow included a stash of food. I bought tea bags, packages of Chinese noodle soup, four loaves of French bread, and peanut butter.

I needed a visa for Russia, which was a pain in the butt to get. It reinforced the sham and racket of getting permission to travel on this planet. I tempered that thought with something Vassily had said: "Mental freedom is much more important than physical freedom." I told him I wanted both, and he laughed for a long time.

Right on schedule, we began to move. The car I was assigned to was divided into compartments with four beds in each. Mine, luckily, was an upper bunk. In the passageway were fold-down chairs where I sat at the window taking in the passing scenery.

We chugged out of Beijing and into the countryside. At noon we stopped at a station with vendors on the platform. I had two dollars in Chinese money that would soon be useless, so I bought twelve large bottles of beer. I drank two, since they were cold. The rest wouldn't stay that way, but on a long train trip, warm beer was better than no beer.

MONGOLIA

The train crossed into Mongolia and headed for the capital of Ulaan Baatar. The landscape changed to the vast, sloping grassland called "the steppes." I pictured Genghis Khan and his Mongol hordes thundering across them to conquer and plunder.

My time on the train fell into a routine. At daylight, with a hot cup of tea in hand, I headed straight for the window to watch the view. When the train made a scheduled stop, I'd get off and walk around the station platform. It got dark at ten o'clock, so I'd go to the dining car for an evening meal. Afterward I'd go to bed and then wake up at daylight and head for the window.

RUSSIA

In Russia the terrain changed to mountains with pine forests. We skirted the huge Lake Baikal, the deepest lake in the world. It supposedly contains one-fifth of the fresh water on the planet, so it must be deep.

There was a cosmopolitan mixture of Chinese, Russians, and Westerners traveling on the train. I became friends with Ken and Debbie, a young couple who were heading home to Ireland. Ken loaned me his copy of Roddy Doyle's new book *The Snapper*, which I read at night by the dim bed light. It was as funny as his first book, *The Commitments*, which was made into a great movie.

Irkutsk, the largest city on the trip, was halfway to Moscow. I celebrated the milestone with a bottle of warm beer.

In a conversation, Vassily had once conveyed to me, "You have only one explicit choice to make in your life. You can either live with the ego-controlled mind or with your higher mind. It's either the insanity of the everyday world or the freedom your higher mind leads to."

Another friend I made on the train was Herbert from Holland. He was traveling with his wife and daughter. At a stop, we went to see if there was anyone selling fresh fruit on the platform. To get there, we had to scramble over seven rows of empty tracks. We found an elderly woman selling wild strawberries, and we each bought a bag. We noticed a freight train was traveling on a track between us and our train. If our train started to leave, we'd be in trouble. Herbert freaked out and started running up and down the platform. I decided that the freight train was moving slowly enough that I could pull myself up on it, climb to the other side, jump off, and maybe catch our departing train.

Since it couldn't be done with a bag of strawberries in my hand, I gobbled them down. Finally, the freight train passed by and Herbert headed straight back to our train. I collected the strawberries he'd dropped, bought another for myself, and got aboard just as we began to leave.

Everything I saw from the train was fascinating: the mountains, the hills, the rolling countryside, and the villages. The towns we passed through were Tayshet, Krasnoyarsk, Novosibirsk, Omsk, Tyumen, Sverdlovsk, Perm, Nizhny Novgorod, and, after a week of the best train ride I'd been on, Moscow.

I had no idea where to stay, but Herbert had taken care of it for me. He introduced me to Andrew, who had two rooms in a student apartment available. The students were on vacation. There was one large room for his family and a small one for me. It cost eight dollars and was a short walk to Red Square!

Herbert and his family were also avid walkers, so we set out immediately to see the sights. I'd seen news films of military parades crossing Red Square, but it wasn't preparation enough for personally setting foot on it. The first thing to get my attention was the famous St. Basil's Cathedral located on the far end. Over five hundred years old, it was unique with its colorful onion-shaped domes.

We walked across the square to Lenin's tomb. We took a look at the guy, and I recognized him but thought he looked like another wax figure.

Behind Lenin's tomb was a high wall that ran the length of the square. On the other side was the Kremlin. I always thought it housed powerful government offices, but there was more to it. We purchased a handful of cheap tickets to enter everything in the large compound, except the government buildings. We saw old cathedrals and churches; ornately designed, sumptuous palaces; museums containing treasures collected by the church and state; gardens, cool and peaceful; and nineteen wall towers, one of which was facing Red Square and had an hourly chiming clock.

One morning, we took a ferry up the Moscow River. It wound through the city, passing Gorky Park. We got off near Ulitsa Arbat, a street with a long outdoor market. Vendors lined the pavement, selling everything from old artifacts to new art.

That afternoon, we ran into Ken and Debbie from the train trip. They were leaving the next day, so Ken gave me his Russian phrase book. It had his address in it and would be returned if I ever made it to Dublin.

The phrase book came in handy. We wanted to tour the Moscow Metro (subway), but all of the signs were in Cyrillic script. We used the book to phonetically pronounce the station names and find our way around.

Most of the large metro stations doubled as air-raid shelters. A project started by Stalin also turned some of them into exquisite works of art. Beautiful mosaics, frescoes and marble artistry made them more like galleries than subway stops.

After Herbert and his family left for Holland, I was on my own. I wandered the back streets and was able to see the day-to-day life of the Muscovites. Moscow had been off-limits for so long, and here I was strolling around like nothing had happened.

I was reminded of what Vassily had said about change. "What was meant by 'your life is a projection from your own subconscious' is that all change is first brought about in the mind. A mental alteration projects to an outer transformation. It's the only way real change outside of you can take place."

I like maps because they not only show where I've been but, more importantly, where I haven't been. I checked my eastern European map, and it revealed a place I'd never been: Poland. My departure was from Moscow's Belorussky Station on the train to Warsaw.

POLAND

Pictures I'd seen of Warsaw were of gray buildings under equally gray skies. It was a surprise to find a bright, warm city with friendly people.

A long walk on each day of my week-long stay in Warsaw led to some unusual places. One was the old town area, which contained the royal castle, a six-hundred-year-old church, and the interesting Rynek Starego Miasta (Old Town Square). It was a large cobblestoned plaza surrounded by restored four-story homes, sidewalk cafés, and shops.

Another unusual find was the Palace of Culture, a tall, Russian-designed, ultra-Gothic building. A rickety elevator took me up thirty floors to a viewing platform with a great view of Warsaw. I saw other places I'd soon visit: the cool and shady Lazienki Park, where I heard an outdoor Chopin piano performance, and a sports stadium on the other side of the wide Vistula River, where a huge traders' market was held.

Wanting to see older Poland, I moved onto Krakow. Walking the narrow streets of the city gave a sense of its age. Over a thousand years old, the essence of it was visible at the interesting and large Rynek Glowny (medieval market square). It was surrounded by old churches and buildings and had a museum in the center. Nearby was the thirteenth-century Royal Wawel Castle. It was closed, but I managed to climb one of the walls and see some of it. Where I stayed was interesting as well: a former convent in an old Augustine Church beside the Vistula River!

A glance at the map showed that Czechoslovakia would be penciled in as the next country on my list. I boarded the train and headed for the Bohemia region and the capital.

CZECHOSLOVAKIA

Prague was exactly what an old European city was supposed to look like. Walking down narrow streets with old buildings and churches was like experiencing history rather than reading about it. The centerpiece was the ninth-century Prague Castle, which was visible from almost everywhere in the city.

I walked the bridge across the Vltava River from Staré Mesto (old town) to the Malá Strona (lesser side). That's where the palaces of the nobility are located. Classic historical squares, churches, palaces, and museums awaited me at every turn. I'd never seen anything like it before.

I also took a train to the town of Plzen, known as the birthplace of pilsner beer. I visited the Museum of Beer Brewing, but entrance to the prominent Pilsner Urquel Brewery was by reservation only. At the main entrance, though, was the brewery pub. I tried a glass, and it was one of the best beers I'd ever tasted. Six pints later, I staggered back to the train. In Prague, I also drank a bottle of the original, authentic, locally made Budweiser beer.

Scanning a map showed me that Hungary was a train ride away. At the station, I drank a final bottle of cold Budvar beer and boarded the train headed for the Hungarian capital.

I continued to put together what I'd learned. I knew the most important undertaking was self-knowledge. And I kept thinking about what Vassily had said that life was a projection from my subconscious. But what was the end result of it all?

HUNGARY

At the train station in Budapest was a group of students touting places to stay. They took me to a six-story university dormitory that was empty for summer vacation. From my window on the fifth floor, I could see the Danube River, Castle Hill, the stately Gellert Hotel, and the old Pest Market Hall.

Budapest was similar to Prague and equally impressive in its centuries-old medieval appearance. It took me days to walk all of Castle Hill, which was full of museums and old buildings. I spent a refreshing day at the Gellert Hotel thermal baths. They're located in the basement of the old structure, which reminded me more of a castle or cathedral.

After ten days, everyone in the student dormitory was told to check out. The rooms had to be readied for the returning students. That prompted a look at the map and the purchase of a ticket to Bulgaria.

BULGARIA

The train arrived in the capital of Sofia in the afternoon. Two steps onto the platform, a young man asked if I needed a place to stay. He was an employee at a university dormitory, also on summer vacation. Although not in a great location — the campus was four miles away — the price was right.

Sofia was a clean, slow-moving city with good areas for walking. It was a little difficult to find my way around, as all the signs used the same Cyrillic script as the Russians.

The highlight of my stay was a ride on the ski lift to the top of Mount Vitosha. Operated year-round, it provided a great view of the city. Another find was the tasty Bulgarian wine.

I took a train to Veliko Turnovo, the old capital of Bulgaria, where I visited the ruins of Tsarevets Citadel Castle, which contained the old royal palace. At night there was an impressive light-and-sound show focused on the ruins.

I found Varna to be a cleaner-than-expected port city on the Black Sea coast. From there, I was eager to ride the hydrofoil forty miles north to Nesebar. Located on a small island-like peninsula, the first settlement at Nesebar was nearly 2,500 years ago. Still visible were ruins from Hellenistic Greece, the Byzantine Empire, and the Ottoman rulers. I walked every narrow street in and around the historic town.

A local bus took me to the tourist area of Sunny Beach, and a second bus on to the larger port city of Burgas. The only thing I did there was go to the movies. I paid twenty-five cents to watch *The Fisher King*. As I was watching the credits at the end of the movie, I noticed that the location manager was a guy I'd known back in Portland.

My vague itinerary was to return to Sofia and revisit Greece. But that idea changed when the map showed how close Burgas was to Turkey. Since I'd never been to Istanbul, the adjustment was easily made.

At the bus station, I bought a ticket for the ten-hour overnight bus to Istanbul. I had a question, though: Why did it take so long to go two hundred miles?

The answer was the crowded, understaffed border crossing located in the middle of nowhere. It was excruciatingly slow and another border fiasco! Nothing could be done about it, so I made the best of the situation by closely observing the craziness.

TURKEY

Early in the morning, we rolled into the three-thousand-year-old former capital of the civilized world. Istanbul is divided into two cultures: Middle Eastern and European. They're separated by the Strait of Bosporus, which connects the Black Sea to the Sea of Marmara, which itself is connected to the Aegean Sea and the Mediterranean by the Dardanelles.

Close to my hotel were the beautifully domed Sancta Sofia (Church of Divine Wisdom) and the Blue Mosque, named for its blue-tiled walls. East meets West in Istanbul.

I also visited the Topkapi Palace. For centuries, it was where the sultan rulers lived. My favorite area was the Harem, with its plush bedrooms.

Nearby was the fascinating Kapali Çarsisi, better known as the Grand Bazaar. I spent days wandering through the colorful market maze. Of the thousands of shops, the most prominent were the vendors selling beautiful handwoven carpets and, my favorite, those that sold cups of thick, black Turkish coffee.

Ten days into my stay in Istanbul, it was decision time. While contemplating where to go, I happened to see a handwritten sign in a travel-agency window.

"It's a charter flight," the agent explained, "returning to Bergamo, Italy, with five empty seats. I didn't expect to sell them, but I put that sign in the window anyway. Since it leaves tomorrow, you can have fifty percent off the already low price."

Flying to northern Italy was cheaper than going overland to Greece, where I'd go later. It also meant I could visit the sergeant from my job in California. He'd told me to stop by if I was in the area. So I flew to Bergamo for pocket change!

There was more to the projection situation than I thought. Vassily had explained that the steps to full awareness did not come in any particular order or fashion. He'd also said, "You'll be surprised at how deeply this delves into your subconscious, and how it reflects all your problems into your outer life. That's when you can begin to extricate yourself from the illusive mess."

ITALY

After the plane landed in Bergamo, I changed some money and was given a shock: the Italian lira was up 30 percent. The dollar had been dropping, but I didn't think it had dropped by that much. My train ticket cost a third more than it had the month before.

It was a picturesque train ride through northern Italy. We passed by lush, green countryside, farmland, and small villages and towns. One thing caught my eye: most of the houses had a small grape vineyard growing near them.

I arrived at the small town south of the air base and called my former boss, the sergeant. He said he wasn't surprised that I'd taken him up on his offer. He let me stay in the airmen's living quarters and gave me a good tour of the area.

He also invited me to his work section's annual barbecue party, which included the local employees. The airmen were drinking cans of American beer, but I noticed the Italian civilian workers each had a bottle of wine. I learned they all had small vineyards and made their own.

They offered me some, and it was pretty damn good. They wanted me to try a glass from each bottle and pick the best. I agreed, but eight glasses later, the decision was thrown out the window: the judge was hammered!

The dollar exchange with the lira had dropped to more than 40 percent. That made travel in Italy even more expensive.

An alternate route to Greece was south through the old Yugoslavia, like I'd done on the Magic Bus tour. The problem was that it had been divided into smaller countries, and there was a war going on between some of them. After checking a map, I thought it could be done anyway. And so what if three different groups of ignorant people wanted to fight each other? They'd get no sympathy from me. Besides, the exciting part of traveling is the travel itself. Figuring out how to get someplace, step-by-step, was what it was all about!

For step one, I left in the morning and went east by train to Trieste on the Italian border.

SLOVENIA and CROATIA

Step two was a bus through the beautiful mountains of Slovenia to its capital, Ljubljana.

Step three was an afternoon bus from Ljubljana to Zagreb, the capital of Croatia. I asked about trains to Belgrade, the capital of Serbia, but there weren't any. The Croats disliked the Serbs and vice versa. So while the war was going on, travel between the countries had been suspended.

At an information booth in the train station, a very nice lady told me there was a bus that went from Croatia into Hungary. It then skirted along the border until there was a place it could enter Serbia. By using a neutral third country, it averted direct travel between the two.

SERBIA

Step four consisted of taking that bus from Zagreb into Hungary and then into Serbia to the town of Subotica.

Step five was a hundred miles by train to Belgrade. I wanted to keep going, as I figured it'd be more difficult for the trigger-happy Serbs to shoot a moving target.

So step six was the first train out of town. That train went to Nis, where it arrived between late at night and early in the morning.

MACEDONIA

At daybreak, step seven was a slow train to Skopje, the capital of Macedonia.

That was followed by step eight, the first train bound for the northern Greek city of Thessaloniki.

GREECE

Step nine occurred with perfect timing. I got off the train in Thessaloniki and boarded another one. It left five minutes later for the overnight trip to Athens. There was a problem, though. I didn't have time to buy a ticket, and I only had about three dollars' worth of Greek drachmas on me. When the conductor asked for my ticket, I gave him all my drachmas, smiled, shrugged my shoulders, and said, "Athens." Without even counting the money, he handed me a ticket and smiled back.

My travel to Greece was a nine-step journey that took three days and covered seven countries and a war zone. Maybe it was done the hard way, but it was the kind of travel I loved!

My travel complications mirrored my difficulties in putting together the metaphysical concepts I'd learned. I recalled Vassily saying that the projected reflection we see is an illusion we mentally create. It fit with the Buddhist teaching that the world we see is *maya*, or illusion. I'd laughed and said, "There's more, or is it less, to this than meets the eye!"

In Athens I discovered that the bus, trolley and subway workers were on strike. I ended up walking four miles to a hostel near the Plaka.

I contacted my friend Sam. He was writing a column in the local English newspaper, composing poetry, appearing in a film or TV commercial from time to time, and providing *I Ching* consultations for his faithful clients.

It was time to look for another country to visit. I hadn't planned on it, but its uniqueness convinced me to visit Israel. The best way to get there was by ship. I booked passage on the *Vergina* for the three-day voyage across the Mediterranean.

Our first stop was the island of Rhodes. During the six-hour layover, I visited the medieval Crusader Castle and ate lunch in the *chora* (old town). I walked through the port city and returned to the ship just before it shoved off.

CYPRUS

The following morning, the ship pulled into port at the city of Limassol on the island of Cyprus. There was an eight-hour layover, so the passengers took taxis the three miles to the city center. I decided to walk and see what was in between.

While strolling along, I noticed there was a familiar aroma in the air, a yeasty odor. And then it hit me: "I smell a brewery!" Sure enough, behind some trees was the Keo beer brewery. At the entrance, I joined a friendly group just starting a tour. When it was over, I spent an enjoyable afternoon drinking free beer in the tasting room and then staggered back to the ship.

ISRAEL

We docked at the main Israeli port of Haifa and the unfriendly immigration officials gave me a three-month visa.

I wanted to check out a kibbutz. It's a community settlement, usually agricultural, run on collective principles. I went to the main kibbutz office in Tel Aviv to learn more. They told me most volunteers were in their twenties, but there was a shortage at the moment. So I was sent to kibbutz Yad Mordecai, near Ashkelon, for an interesting stay.

At Yad Mordecai, volunteers were given bare-essentials accommodation, meals, and $150 a month for toiling six days a week. The work was agricultural, in orange, avocado, corn, and honey production. My job, however, was at the kibbutz store, in charge of stocking all of the perishables — fruits, vegetables, eggs, milk, and the like.

Most of the kibbutzniks were friendly, but a few were hostile toward foreigners. I never figured out why. The volunteers, though, were another story. The young men and women were Danes, Swedes, Aussies, Kiwis from New Zealand, Zims from Zimbabwe, RSAs from South Africa, and a couple of Yanks. They were a friendly, happy group.

During the week, we all diligently did our jobs, but come Friday, the night before the weekly Jewish Shabbat and a day off, it was kick-out-the-jams party time! Whether it was in the bomb shelter turned kibbutz pub, the dilapidated recreation room, or around a big, late-night bonfire, it was a drinking, dancing, singing, laughing, hell-raising time.

I stayed at the kibbutz for two and a half months. The two weeks left on my visa gave me enough time to visit Jerusalem, the so-called holy city, before going to Egypt.

The area of Jerusalem that attracts the most attention is the old walled city. It's divided into Muslim, Christian, and Jewish sections. Inside were some fascinating places, like the Temple Mount, holy to all three religions and, therefore, posing an interesting predicament. I did give each of the three faiths equal time by visiting the Jewish Western Wall, the Muslim Dome of the Rock, and the Christian Via Dolorosa. But I wasn't moved enough to sign up with any of them.

What I was moved to do was figure out how what I'd learned came together metaphysically. I tried using my higher mind to get answers, especially concerning this illusion thing. I got some odd results, too. For example, if everything is a projected illusion, that answers the big question about whether god made it. But why it was an illusion remained unanswered.

The hostel I stayed in offered an all-day tour to the Dead Sea area. The first stop was Masada, the mountaintop fortress built two thousand years ago. It gained fame in the first century CE when a thousand Jewish zealots held off the Roman army for five months and then, instead of submitting to capture, committed suicide.

We then went to the lowest spot on the planet. With eight times more salt than the ocean, it is impossible to sink in the Dead Sea. Bobbing up and down on the surface was definitely a strange sensation.

The tour's last stop was in the middle of Israel's dry Judean desert at the lush, green oasis of Ein Gedi. After a visit to the cooling waterfall, we returned to Jerusalem.

My visa was about to expire, so it was time to move on. There was a seldom-used border crossing near the Israeli Red Sea resort city of Eilat. After a five-hour bus trip from Jerusalem, I crossed into the Sinai Peninsula and the North African country of Egypt.

EGYPT

The only way to get from the border to Dahab, a hundred miles south, was by bus, which had already left, or a shared taxi. Five other travelers and I chose the latter.

Dahab was a budget resort on the Red Sea's Gulf of Aqaba. It was difficult to spend more than seven dollars a day on a place to stay and a couple of meals. Visitors were also attracted to diving in the waters around the coral reef and access to marijuana. Pot was easily purchased from young boys at the small beach. Some of the guests called it paradise.

I became friends with Jim and Denise, a couple from London. The three of us wanted to visit the Nile Valley, so we decided to share transportation expenses.

The journey was divided into three stages. First we departed Dahab in a shared taxi. Our destination was sixty miles across the desert at Sharm el-Sheikh on the southern tip of the Sinai Peninsula. Next we boarded the small ferry bound for Hurghada on the other side of the Red Sea. The final stage of the trip was a four-hour drive, in another shared taxi, to one of the best ancient places I'd ever been to.

It's now called Luxor, but when it served as the early capital of Egypt, it was known as Thebes. In the center of town was the main structure of the old civilization, the Luxor Temple. There were huge, tall columns throughout it, with large statues of King Ramses II guarding them. At night, strategically placed lights lit it up, and it stood in stark contrast to the nearby dark River Nile. Close by was the excellent Luxor Museum, with displays of interior furnishings, jewelry, pottery, and statues of the pharaohs.

Two miles down the road, and just as imposing, was the enormous Karnak Temple. It was built and added onto over the centuries. It contains hundreds of huge decorated columns that once supported its roof. Trying to figure out which king built what was complicated, but the farther into it I went, the older it got. It also had a good nighttime light-and-sound show, during which the history of Thebes was told.

We crossed the Nile to the west bank and the Valley of the Kings, where temples honoring entombed pharaohs are located. The most notable were Tutankhamun and the Ramses kings. Most of the tombs had hidden cave entrances with corridors leading down into vast halls and decorated burial chambers. My favorite was Seti I, as it had the most colorful and vivid paintings and best relief sculptures. The Valley of the Queens was also interesting, as were the Temple of Hatshepsut and the Ramasseum.

Jim, Denise, and I wanted to see the statues at Abu Simbel, so we took a bus 130 miles south to Aswan. Another 180 miles farther was the southernmost part of Egypt and Abu Simbel. Out in the middle of nowhere are four colossal and impressive statues of the self-deified pharaoh, King Ramses II. They were carved from one gigantic rock as a monument to him and Queen Nefertari.

There's an additional modern-day twist to Abu Simbel. Due to the Aswan Dam, Lake Nasser was threatening to flood the entire place. In a massive feat of engineering skill, all of the statues and temples were sectioned, moved to higher ground and pieced back together, out of harm's way.

After a week in Aswan, we headed north to Cairo. With fifteen million people, it's the largest city in Africa, and even though it was chaotic, there was a lot to see.

The Egyptian Museum was amazing. The main draw was the funerary treasure from the tomb of the boy king Tutankhamun. There were thousands of statues of kings, queens, and gods; there were mummies, coffins, and sarcophagi of pharaohs; there was an amazing amount of dazzling gold jewelry; and there was a large wooden boat that transported the soul of a pharaoh. I didn't leave until forced out at closing time.

Located on the other side of the Nile were the three pyramids at Giza and the Sphinx. Five thousand years old, they're known as one of the seven wonders of the ancient world. I spent an initial half hour just staring at them. At the pyramid of Cheops, the largest in Egypt, I was able to climb down inside and see the king's chamber. The pyramid of Chephren was also good for interior exploration. The pyramid of Mycerinus was the smallest of the three. What was mind-boggling, though, was the number of huge stone blocks needed to build them.

Then there's the nearby mysterious Sphinx: a lion with the head of a man. Its forgotten purpose is the fodder for stories and superstitions.

The entire country was incredible. If you've never been to Egypt and seen that ancient civilization, you've missed out.

ISRAEL

After ten days in Cairo, I was on a bus headed back to Israel. I revisited Yad Mordecai Kibbutz, and they told me to get back to work. I laughed, said shalom, and left!

I took a bus to Haifa and booked passage on the ship back to Greece. After another rude encounter with Israeli immigration officials, I departed.

CYPRUS

While on deck, gazing at the reflection of the sky on the blue Mediterranean Sea, I contemplated something Vassily had said. He'd answered my question about how reflection worked by stating, "It's a subconscious image projected out like a movie to make it look like a real outside world." In a Buddhist dhamma talk, a monk had defined illusion as a mental image viewed as reality. They fit together, but a full understanding and realization were not yet mine.

At Limassol, I revisited the Keo brewery. There's something about free beer that made me want to return. On the second day was another stop at the island of Rhodes, and on the third day we steamed into the Greek port of Piraeus.

GREECE

Back in Athens, I contacted my friend Sam. He suggested I visit the agency he'd been using for film and TV work. They sent me to an audition, and I was cast in two commercials for a Greek bank. It was fun, and it put a few drachmas in my pocket, too.

It wasn't long before I was wondering where to go next. The hostel where I stayed had a travel agency with a notice offering a one-way flight to London for a very low price. It was another charter flight with four open seats, one of which became mine.

ENGLAND

After the plane landed at Heathrow, I phoned Pete, my friend from traveling in India. He insisted I billet myself at his home in Lewisham.

Pete was leaving on another trip to India in three days, but he said I was welcome to stay and keep an eye on his place. I told him he might see me again when he returned in seven weeks.

I enjoyed London all over again: from the British Museum and the National Gallery to the hip Soho area and everything in between. I went to a different pub every night, to the movies, and to a blues concert, and I got together with Jim and Denise, my friends from Egypt.

It was winter in England, and so cold I'd speak Spanish to warm up. That gave me the idea to go to Spain for the warmer climate. In a city-guide magazine, I saw an ad for an inexpensive one-way charter flight to Alicante, Spain.

SPAIN

Alicante, on the Mediterranean coast, is known for its Costa Blanca tourist area. Another attraction was the historical Castillo de Santa Barbara, an old fort on top of a hill. It offered great views of the city, port, and beaches below.

I went farther north to Valencia, and the timing of my visit couldn't have been better. Las Fallas, which meant "the fires" in local lingo, was an annual week-long festival. It included fireworks, parades, bullfights, parties, and exhibits of huge wood-and-plaster comical statues. There were about three hundred of them, and each neighborhood had one. Some mocked famous people or current events, while others were in-jokes for the locals, but all were artistic and fascinating. Then, on the last night, each one was torched and turned into a roaring bonfire.

I'd heard that Córdoba is one of Spain's oldest cities. Its main attraction is the Mezquita (mosque), which was built in the eighth century by the invading Moors. The huge building took up several square blocks. The plain exterior was deceptive, as the true beauty of it was inside. The columns, pillars, arches, and ornate ceiling were all of exquisite Moorish design.

Nearby was the five-hundred-year-old Alcazar castle. It's where the Catholic monarchs headquartered the brutal Inquisition. I was glad to have missed that event.

After a week in Córdoba, I took the train to Seville. Santa Maria de la Sede, the largest Catholic cathedral in Spain, is located there. It's also the largest Gothic building in the world. The complex contains the famous Giralda Towers and remnants of an old mosque built by the Moors during the five hundred years they were in town. The tomb of Christopher Columbus was supposedly there as well.

Seville was crowded, so it was easy to leave, especially since my next stop was Jerez de la Frontera. Jerez means "sherry," and this is the best region in the world for its production.

I stayed at a large hostel with only six guests. One of them, a Canadian girl, and I decided to go on a tour of a sherry bodega. We were given information on the aging process, saw lots of big barrels, and visited a tasting room.

I'm not a sherry drinker — it's too sweet for me — and my Canadian friend, being a true "hoser," was a beer drinker. In any case, that afternoon we were left alone in the tasting room. So we indulged. There were about forty different bottles of sherry, and we sampled nearly all of them. Some were better than others, but halfway through they all tasted the same!

Leaving Jerez by bus, I traveled to the southernmost point of Spain and the seedy port city of Algeciras. The huge Rock of Gibraltar could be seen just down the road.

Another bus took me along the Costa del Sol resort area of Marbella to Málaga. It's the largest city in the region and had some good walks. The best was uphill to the Alcazaba, a fortress dating back to the eighth century. Through the years, it was made into a sizable stronghold. Above it, on top of Gibralfaro Hill, was a great view of the city and port.

That vista provided a problem for me with the illusion thing. Like the view, everything looked real to me. Vassily had replied to my enquiry concerning that with, "Oh, yes, it looks real. Your ego and subconscious are very good at creating a mentally projected illusion. It's to keep you distracted and occupied."

My travel through Spain took me to Granada, three hours north of Málaga by bus. I remembered reading that it was once the finest city on the Iberian Peninsula. The remaining proof was the best old palace I'd ever seen.

The Alhambra Palace was home to Muslim rulers for centuries, but eventually it became the last residence and fortification of the defeated Moors. Inside its walls were lush patios, pools of water, flowered gardens, large halls, and elaborately decorated chambers, all of it in exquisite Moorish architectural design. Climbing to the top of a watchtower provided a great view of Granada, with the Sierra Nevada as a backdrop. Nearby was El Generalife, the equally ornate summer palace of the sultans.

When I departed, it was on a train from the old Moorish capital to the modern Spanish capital.

Madrid is a big city with lots of museums, large parks, and plazas. But I walked around with no agenda, looking at whatever was in my path. I found a small tailor shop where I had a button sewn on my shirt and a bakery where I ate some delicious pastries. The only way to find these places was to go and look. And that's what I did every day of my week-long stay.

I moved on for a short stay in Barcelona. I visited Las Ramblas, the long street through the center of the city. There were numerous cafés for lunch, a quick cup of coffee, or a leisurely glass of wine. I didn't stay long, though, because my next destination was the French Riviera!

FRANCE

My initial stop was in Nice on the Cote d'Azur, or French Riviera. It was a relaxed and easygoing city with good beaches. "The beaches are nice in Nice!"

I went on two day-trips. One was to Monaco to see the palace and casino at Monte Carlo and the other to Cannes, where I saw expensive five-star hotels and their private beaches.

Before returning to London, I wanted to visit Paris and the Eiffel Tower. I'd seen the "City of Lights" in numerous French films and had always wanted to visit it.

I enjoyed walking through the narrow side streets and down wide avenues. The most impressive was Avenue des Champs Elysees, which was a mile long and ended at the Arc de Triomphe.

Located next to the Seine River, the Eiffel Tower was no longer the tallest structure in the world. But it was over a hundred years old, and that added to its stature. I wanted to climb to the top, but it wasn't allowed. I did take the stairs to the second and third levels, but it was by the mandatory elevator the rest of the way to the top.

I arrived at the viewing platform in the late afternoon of a clear day, and the view was stupendous. There was Paris stretched out in every direction as far as the eye could see. It was incredible. I thought about a second ascent the following day, but it would have been anticlimactic. Instead, I bought a ticket for the ferry and bus trip back to London.

While alone on the ferry back to England, I realized I needed to know more about subconscious projection and illusion. I just didn't comprehend how projection happened and how it affected me — or how I affected it. From my stay at the Buddhist monastery, I remembered learning that Buddha's final temptation was overcoming *maya*, or illusion. But that didn't help me figure it out.

ENGLAND

I again stayed with Pete, who'd just returned from India. He asked if I knew anything about cricket. I didn't, but I was interested. He explained the rules and took me to see a professional match at the Oval stadium. It was like baseball, but the play went a lot slower. Pete thought I knew enough and asked me to play in a weekend match with a group of his friends. I managed to score a couple of runs and played well enough in the field to help our side.

While traveling I'd kept in touch with Bryan, my friend in Hong Kong. A letter from him had arrived at Pete's, in which he described having a job dealing with electronics. He asked if I was interested in working, too. I wrote back asking for details and when to show up. Returning to the Far East sounded good, since I'd gone as far west in Europe as possible. Or had I?

A letter from Hong Kong would take a couple of weeks, so I decided to go to Ireland for a pint of authentic Guinness!

A combined bus-and-ferry round-trip ticket to Dublin cost less than the fare for the ferry alone. It seemed strange, but I paid and got on the bus. After arriving in Holyhead, Wales, it took four hours to cross the Irish Sea. Another short bus ride, and I was finally in Dublin.

IRELAND

It was Friday evening by the time I'd checked into a hostel, showered, and was ready to go out. I had the address of Ken and Debbie, my friends from the trip to Moscow, but I'd wait until the following day to visit them.

My plan for the evening was to take a look at Dublin. It was a six-block stroll to the central O'Connell Street. I walked the bridge over the River Liffey to the Temple Bar district on the south side. Then it finally dawned on me: I hadn't quaffed a real Guinness yet! But I just happened to be in front of a likely place to remedy the situation.

It was an Irish pub that had clearly been at that location for a number of years. I walked under a sign that read "McDaids" and went in. I was at the bar, ready to order, when I noticed a picture of a familiar face on the wall.

"That's Brendan Behan!" I said out loud.

The barman told me this was his favorite pub and that he'd done much of his writing at a table in the corner and even once helped paint the place. I told him I'd been in a play he wrote.

"You won't believe this," I said. "I just got to Ireland, I've been in Dublin two hours, it's finally time for my first pint of real Guinness, and I was guided to this pub. Is that what they call the luck of the Irish?"

With a knowing smile, the barman poured my pint. When the glass was full, he slowed the tap down and, with the very narrow stream of dark stout, he drew a shamrock on top of the foam.

I quickly downed the pint.

"Hey, you're supposed to take your time drinking a Guinness. Just sip it."

"This is my first pint of the real stuff," I said. "And I'm twice your age. I'd say I've got a lot of catchin' up to do."

"And another pint for ya!" said the laughing barman.

The next day I went to the address Ken and Debbie had given me. There was a surprised look on Ken's face when he saw me at the door with his Russian phrase book in hand.

They insisted I stay with them, as they had an extra bedroom. Just two days in the country and I'd discovered Irish luck and hospitality!

During the following week, Ken and I went on several excursions. The first was a visit to the Guinness brewery. The tour was through a museum where they showed a couple of films: one on the brewing process and another of the fascinating coopers (barrel makers). At the end, you're allowed to drink two pints of fresh Guinness, but they weren't counting, so we continued to drink. Eventually they noticed, and we were told to stagger out.

The following day we went to a pub in Howth, a small, picturesque fishing village a few miles up the coast from Dublin. The day after, Ken took me to the authentic horse traders' market. The buyers and sellers were characters right out of an Irish storybook.

On Sunday we went to the Gaelic Football County Finals at Croke Park. With ninety thousand cheering fans watching, Dublin barely defeated Donegal in the Super Bowl of Ireland.

As a special treat, Ken let me watch a tape of the BBC production of Roddy Doyle's book *The Snapper*. It was an insightful, hilarious look at Irish life and times.

Wanting to see more of Ireland, I went on a four-day visit to Killarney. From the bus, the view of the countryside, rolling hills, and farmland included every shade of green imaginable.

In Killarney, the locals were extremely friendly. They always had time to chat, give directions, or point out their favorite pub.

I went on a bus tour around the Ring of Kerry, the circle road on the spectacular Kerry peninsula. It's also the farthest western point in Europe, so I'd finally gone as far as possible!

I returned to Dublin, thanked Ken and Debbie for their hospitality, had a last pint of Guinness, and headed to the port.

While viewing the Irish Sea from a deck of the ferry, I recalled Vassily asking me, "Have you ever had an instantaneous, clear revelation? If you quiet the incessant thoughts, your higher mind will have an easier time communicating with you."

I decided to do exactly that, as I needed answers to the subconscious, reflection, projection, and illusion questions.

ENGLAND

Pete had never been to Ireland, so I gave him the scoop on the place: "If you like Guinness and friendly people, you have to go!"

A letter from Bryan had arrived. He said he was flying between Hong Kong, Taipei, and Tokyo and delivering electronic accessories. It was like being an air courier, and the pay was good. He added that I should get there as soon as possible and gave me a phone number to call when I arrived.

I bought a low-priced one-way ticket to Hong Kong, via Moscow on Russia's Aeroflot Airlines. Before paying, I asked what kind of plane it was. I don't think I'd have made the purchase if they were using one of the Russian-made Illyushin or Tupalov aircraft that had recently been falling from the sky; they assured me the plane was a European-made Airbus.

It was 1993, and after more than two years and twenty-five countries, I was going back to Asia. That was fine with me, but the questions remained: Was there more to the metaphysical puzzle, and was there an ultimate answer?

CHAPTER FOURTEEN

"Truth, like history, is whatever those in power say it is."
— MIKE RESTIVO

"You will know the truth, and the truth shall set you free."
—JESUS

"THAT High Drayt planet was different," I said. "Imagine living your life completely submerged. I wonder if they have waterbeds."

"Michael, you come up with some odd observations."

"Thanks, Captain. Now I'd like to hear about that other Earthling. You said he was a great teacher, but he was misrepresented. What's that about?"

"It's about what he taught. Then, after his life ended, distorted and contrived stories were told about him."

"What kind of stories?"

"Let me start at the beginning. He was born about two thousand Earth years ago and given the name Yeshua. He lived in Nazareth, a small town located on a popular trade route. That road began in Asia, went through India and the Middle East, and then to Egypt. It ended in Alexandria, the intellectual and cultural center on the planet at that time. Travelers and traders would often stop for the night in Nazareth, and the curious boy would visit them."

"That's a good way to meet interesting people," I said.

"To identify some of the travelers," continued the Captain, "I'm going to regress a bit. In India, there was a war-waging king named Asoka who realized the truths of Buddhism. He changed his ways and began living the doctrine of the Buddha.

"King Asoka wanted to spread this liberating teaching, so he sent monks out on the trade route. The open-minded people of Alexandria accepted them, and a Buddhist monastery was built. The monks were admired because they taught with kindness and compassion, and they healed the sick. It was from the traveling monks that Yeshua heard of the Buddha's teaching.

"As a young boy, he visited the monastery. His understanding of Buddhism amazed the monks. Seeing he had the mind and heart of Buddha himself, they suggested he travel to India to learn more.

"At the age of thirteen, Yeshua made the long journey to northeast India where the Buddha had lived. During his extended stay in the area, he had a realization that went beyond Buddhism. He called it the Miracle of Forgiveness. It wasn't the mundane forgiveness of transgressions on the Earthly level. It was a deeper forgiveness that brought freedom from the ego and its control of the subconscious."

"That sounds interesting," I thought out loud.

"When Yeshua arrived back at the monastery in Alexandria, it was obvious to the monks that a great teacher was in their midst.

"Seventeen years after his departure, at the age of thirty, Yeshua returned to the land of his birth to enlighten the people living there.

"He'd been in his homeland three years, and his understanding of the Miracle of Forgiveness expanded. He recognized that a mental projection from his subconscious created the illusion of an outer life, and it was controlled by the ego. He realized an ingenious way humans could retrain their minds and be free of the ego. Yeshua knew it worked, as he accomplished it and became fully enlightened."

"Just like Buddha!" I exclaimed. "He found another way for

Earthlings to get out of that mess!"

"There was a Jewish festival in the city of Jerusalem, and Yeshua decided to attend and teach. He found a spot off to the side of the festivities and began talking with visitors. Due to the radically different topic, a crowd gathered. The authorities were informed of the commotion and, not wanting any problems during the festival, decided to set an example. As a deterrent, he was arrested and sentenced to crucifixion."

"Cruci-what?"

"Nailed to a cross that was placed in the open so everyone could see it," said the Captain. "The Roman government used it for punishment and humiliation to deter lawbreakers."

"The brutality on that planet is unbelievable," I said.

"The sequence went like this: Yeshua was arrested late at night and placed on the cross early the next morning, and his body ceased functioning a few days later. I was given orders to go to Earth and meet with him."

"So you assisted him in ascending, too?"

"Yes, but he also had a couple of requests. First, he wanted to stay awhile longer, and my first thought was *Here we go again!* But he only wanted to stay long enough to visit his important followers, and I didn't have a problem with that. Yeshua appeared to them, and they were shocked, thinking he was dead. He reminded them that the body and death were an illusion, and that he hadn't experienced any pain or suffering from the crucifixion. They were amazed, but they knew he was speaking the truth.

"After his alleged death, a religion formed utilizing his name and reputation. He never intended for that to happen, but over the years, several groups took advantage. They used the power of the religion as a means to dominate people and countries. They renamed him Jesus and changed many things about his life, death, and teaching.

The present-day religion is unaware of the original, amazing truth that he taught. And that leads me to Yeshua's other request. He wanted access, at a later date, to an Earthling so he could transcribe his complete teaching in detail. He said it would be two thousand Earth years before humans would be able to read and comprehend it."

"So his original teaching to retrain their minds is what's important," I observed. "And it'll free them."

"You got it!" said the Captain.

"Can I hear more about that miracle forgiveness stuff?"

"Michael, you'll learn all about it right after that surprise I mentioned, and that'll happen as soon as we complete our new assignment."

The Captain snapped his fingers and laughed, and a printout of our new orders appeared. He handed it to me to read.

"Let's see. We're to assist new ascenders in sector 4X4 on the square planet, Quebik."

"Oh, yeah," said the smiling Captain. "That's where everyone's been cornered and has to think outside the box."

CHAPTER FIFTEEN

*"Without self knowledge, man cannot be free
and will always remain a slave."* — GURDJIEFF

*"Be careful what you pretend to be because you are
what you pretend to be."* — KURT VONNEGUT

ON THE flight to Hong Kong, I reminisced about my latest travel adventure: I'd been through Asia, Eastern Europe, part of the Middle East and North Africa, and then to land's end in Western Europe, and now I was heading back to Asia.

HONG KONG / JAPAN / TAIWAN

In Hong Kong, I met with Bryan and the boss, a Chinese–Malaysian businessman. Because I had an American passport and could easily go through immigration and customs, he immediately hired me to work as an air courier. I started flying from Hong Kong to Tokyo and Taiwan several times a week.

The traveling certainly helped with my awareness. I realized it wasn't me, or "I," that caught those ego-initiated thoughts when they appeared out of nowhere. It was the awareness that caught them. When those captured thoughts were studied, they revealed more of how the ego was directing my life. Most of those thoughts were opinions or judgments directed at other people and situations. I wanted to understand how that tied in with what Vassily had said about the mental projections from my subconscious.

In a Hong Kong bookstore, I came across a publication on quantum physics. I read a statement attributed to Einstein: "The separation between past, present, and future is only an illusion." I had a question about how that fit in with what I'd already realized. I scoured the library and every bookstore looking for more information on the subject.

Much of what I read about quantum physics was compatible with Buddhism — in particular, the idea that everything happens simultaneously in the present moment. The past and future are an illusion. I determined that, relative to infinity, it had to be true because infinity has no beginning and no end. It is immeasurable and, therefore, it always just is. It just didn't appear that way to our human condition.

I stayed in Hong Kong for two and a half years and never tired of it. Even the crowded conditions didn't bother me. Living in a different culture has always been fun, and I used it as a reminder to wake up and be aware of the moment.

Eventually, the business began to falter, and the boss moved back to Malaysia. I took a final vacation to Thailand and then returned to California. I wondered what was next. Whatever it was, I hoped it'd happen soon and would include the final answer.

CHAPTER SIXTEEN

"You were not placed in the world to wander aimlessly,
but placed to discover the Cosmic Castle."
— VERNON HOWARD

WHEN we'd finished assisting the beings ascending back to reality on the square planet Quebik, I said to the Captain, "I'm ready for that surprise."

"OK," said the Captain with a laugh. "First, I want to thank you for being an excellent assistant, and I appreciate the good company you've provided. But why do you think I told you about the history of Earth and its inhabitants?"

"It's because you became interested in them and their problem. I can tell you really care and would do anything to help them."

"You're right, but there's another reason. You see, Michael, it's because you're an Earthling."

"What? I'm an Earthling! Wow, that is a surprise. I had no idea. You certainly fooled me. But wait, Captain, I have some questions. Like, why and what for, and give me a reason."

"You're a good sport," said the Captain. "And that'll help because now that your assignment with me has been completed, you'll be going back to Earth."

"Why do I have to go back?"

"To be honest, you haven't been gone that long."

"How long has it been?" I managed to ask.

"It's been about the same as a fraction of a second."

"Wait a minute! It seems longer than that to me."

"The Earthlings need the illusion of time," said the Captain, "so they can deal with the problems they have. But out here where the universe crosses over to infinity and pure reality, there is no time. But don't be concerned with the illusion and time thing. You'll learn all about them and a lot more.

"When you rejoin your physical body back on Earth, you won't notice anything different, and you won't remember much of what took place here.

"As for why you have to return, it's because you still have important lessons to learn. There's a reason my story ended when it did. The last person I talked about was Yeshua. As promised, I allowed him access to another Earthling so his teachings could be transcribed into written form. That transcription has been completed and is now available as a book back on Earth."

"So he followed through on the agreement you made with him."

"Yep. And, I might add, the book is brilliantly laid out."

"What's it about?"

"For all intents and purposes, it helps resolve the Earthling's mental predicament. If you recall, Yeshua realized the Miracle of Forgiveness. The book is entitled *A Course in Miracles*, and it contains lessons on retraining the mind and gaining release from the confining mental state humans are experiencing.

"After your return, you'll be guided to the book, and it'll assist you in freeing yourself."

"Before leaving," I said with a lump in my throat, "let me thank you for everything I learned. And it was fun, too. But I have one last question: Will I get to see you again?"

"You will, and already have, as the case may be, but in another form on Earth. You won't recognize me, but there'll be a laugh that'll remind you of me, and it'll make you smile, too. And we'll be united again when you free yourself and are ready to return to true reality."

"I'll definitely look forward to that, and to seeing you again, too," I said wholeheartedly.

CHAPTER SEVENTEEN

"Publication is a self-invasion of privacy."
— MARSHALL McLUHAN

NOT long after my return from my last travel adventure, I went for a Sunday visit to the local Barnes & Noble bookstore. I liked browsing through the periodicals for special or timely articles. But on this particular visit, I walked right past the magazine racks and found myself directly in front of the new-nonfiction bookshelf. I didn't glance over the many books available, though. I looked, or truthfully, stared, at just one: *The Disappearance of the Universe*. The title didn't mean anything to me, but I picked it up and read some of it anyway. What I read immediately stunned me. The book contained insights and revelations that finally put the pieces of the puzzle together for me. More importantly, it described and explained another book entitled *A Course in Miracles*. The "Text," "Workbook for Students," and "Manual for Teachers" took seven years to be transcribed by a dedicated woman. But even more amazing, the words came to her from Jesus. He's returned, but not in the illusion of the flesh. He's returned with the lessons humans can use to retrain their minds.

It was important that I read *The Disappearance of the Universe* first. Otherwise I wouldn't have known exactly what *A Course* was about, and for that I am thankful to its author, Gary Renard. Also, I'm sure he's as thankful as I am that Jesus didn't forget us and that he provided the amazing lessons in *A Course* for everyone.

EPILOGUE

IT'S BEEN a long time since my mind-expanding experience in Golden Gate Park, followed by my magical meeting with Vassily and all my travel adventures. What I learned from them is just as important today. Without them my life would have been one of undiscovered possibilities. I wouldn't have heard Vassily's unique laugh and him saying, "Remember, it's your awareness and higher mind that's important, not the ego."

I also wouldn't have heard the Captain as he laughed and said, "Michael, you come up with some odd observations."

I would have been trapped in an illusion of my own making. My life wouldn't be what it needed to be. And I wouldn't be on the journey Vassily told me I would take because he knew I'd already taken it.

If we can't share with others the realizations and freedom that the wise ones gave us, life — and its journey — is less than it should be. If my experiences in these pages have done nothing else but pass along to you some of Vassily's wisdom, or the notion that life is a journey of learning we only need to agree to make, this book has done what I intended it to do.

May you find your Vassily, may you take your own journey, and may the Captain be with you forever.

Made in the USA
Charleston, SC
26 October 2016